GREAT THEMES IN THEOLOGY

GREAT THEMES
IN THEOLOGY

STUDY PAPERS
PREPARED FOR AMERICAN BAPTIST
THEOLOGICAL CONFERENCES

Edited by

LYNN LEAVENWORTH

THE JUDSON PRESS

CHICAGO / PHILADELPHIA / LOS ANGELES

LIBRARY OF CONGRESS CATALOG CARD NO. 58-9990

Printed in the U.S.A.
for The Judson Press by
American Book–Stratford Press, Inc., New York

FOREWORD

SCORES OF INDIVIDUALS have carried responsibilities for the development of the theological discussions in the American Baptist Convention from which the seven papers in this book have been selected. Adequate acknowledgements are impossible. However, it would be unpardonable not to mention the following. Dr. Edwin T. Dahlberg, now pastor of the Delmar Baptist Church of St. Louis, was the chairman of the Committee of Review which asked the Convention in 1950 to endorse the calling of conferences to discuss theology. Dr. Dahlberg also ably led the discussions at the first Theological Conference in 1954 as chairman of the plenary sessions. Dr. Eugene M. Austin, now President of Colby Junior College, furthered the concern when he read a paper interpreting the need for such conferences at the meeting of the General Council in January, 1952. Dr. Wilbour E. Saunders, chairman of the Board of Education and Publication of the American Baptist Convention and President of the Colgate Rochester

Divinity School, gave personal leadership to the program as chairman of the Central Planning Committee of the Theological Conferences. The following chairmen of the 1956 Regional Theological Conferences guided the preparation of the many papers from which the seven papers were selected: Dr. Eugene M. Austin, Dr. Robert T. Handy, Dr. Winthrop S. Hudson, Dr. W. Alvin Pitcher, and Dr. John E. Skoglund.

The secretarial services of Mrs. Donald J. Simmons have been invaluable throughout the preparation of the papers for both the national and the regional conferences. In addition, grateful acknowledgement is made of her untiring work in the detailed preparation of the present manuscript.

The persons listed above and the many others who remain unmentioned, but who have had a noteworthy share in the development of this material, will consider themselves amply repaid if the seven papers selected for the present volume prove adequate to indicate the direction the discussions have taken and to stimulate interest and concern for continuing studies and discussion.

LYNN LEAVENWORTH
Director, Department of Theological Education
The Board of Education and Publication
The American Baptist Convention

New York, N. Y.
March 1, 1958

CONTRIBUTORS TO THIS BOOK

THE AUTHORS of the papers in this book worked in close collaboration with study committees which were preparing for the American Baptist theological conferences. While they assume full responsibility for their papers, the authors express their deep appreciation to the members of their committees for the contributions of sub-papers and creative discussion.

I. The Biblical Basis of the Gospel
   by WALTER J. HARRELSON, Associate Professor of Old Testament and Dean of the Divinity School of the University of Chicago.

   The Committee included:

   CHARLES R. ANDREWS,   Pastor of the Oak Lawn Baptist Church, Cranston, R. I.

   KENNETH L. MAXWELL,   former Pastor of the Central Baptist Church, Hartford, Conn.; now Executive Director of the Department of International Affairs of the National Council of Churches.

7

SAMUEL H. MILLER, Pastor of the Old Baptist Church, Cambridge, Mass., and Adjunct Professor of Philosophy of Religion at Andover Newton Theological School and Harvard University.

HILLYER H. STRATON, Pastor of the First Baptist Church, Malden, Mass.

God and the Natural Order
by ROBERT B. HANNEN, Professor of Christian Theology and Ethics, Berkeley Baptist Divinity School, Berkeley, Cal.

The Committee included:

CHARLES R. BELL, Pastor of the First Baptist Church, Pasadena, Cal.

JOHN R. JANEWAY, Professor of Theology at the Spanish-American Baptist Seminary.

CLARENCE E. DOWNING, Assistant Professor of Religion at the University of Redlands, Redlands, Cal.

ROBERT KEVORKIAN, Pastor of the First Baptist Church, Anaheim, Cal.

The Eternal Son and The Incarnate Word
by VICTOR F. SCALISE, Pastor of the Calvary Baptist Church, Lowell, Mass.

The Committee included:

RALPH J. BERTHOLF, Pastor of the First Baptist Church, Troy, New York.

WILLIAM H. HAMILTON, Assistant Professor of Christian Theology and Ethics at Colgate Rochester Divinity School, Rochester, New York.

CHRISTIAN B. JENSEN, Pastor of the First Baptist Church, Pittsfield, Mass.

LaRUE A. LOUGHHEAD, Pastor, Hudson Falls Baptist Church, Hudson Falls, New York.

EWALD MAND, Pastor, First Baptist Church, Amherst, Mass.

A Christian Doctrine of Man: Man's Essential Nature
  by W. ALVIN PITCHER, Professor of Social Ethics, Divinity School,
  The University of Chicago, Chicago, Ill.

  The Committee included:

ORA LEE ICE,	Pastor of the Calvary Baptist Church, Minneapolis, Minn.
HAROLD O. MCNEIL,	Pastor of the First Baptist Church, Albert Lea, Minn.
ANTON PEARSON,	Professor of Old Testament Language and Literature at Bethel Seminary, St. Paul, Minn.
PIETER SMIT,	Pastor of the First Baptist Church, St. Paul, Minn.

How God Overcomes Sin: Atonement and Justification
  by ROBERT T. HANDY, Associate Professor of Church History at
  Union Theological Seminary, New York, N.Y.

  The Committee included:

MURRAY J. S. FORD,	former Pastor of the Baptist Church of the Redeemer, Brooklyn, N.Y.
ELMER G. MILLION,	former Executive Director of the Department of the Ministry of the National Council of Churches; now Director of the Department of Schools and Colleges of the Board of Education and Publication of the American Baptist Convention.
ROBERT W. SPIKE,	former Pastor of the Judson Memorial Church, New York, N.Y.; now of Home Mission Board, Congregational Christian Church.
GEORGE D. YOUNGER,	Pastor of Mariner's Temple, New York, N.Y.

A Baptist Theology of Church Order
  by HARRY H. KRUENER, Dean of the Chapel, Denison University,
  Granville, Ohio.

The Committee included:

HARVEY COX,	With the Y.M.C.A., Oberlin College, Oberlin, Ohio.
V. E. DEVADUTT,	Professor of Ecumenical Theology and Missions at Colgate Rochester Divinity School, Rochester, New York.
HOWARD R. MOODY,	Pastor, Judson Memorial Church, New York, N.Y.

Christ and Man's Hope
  by CHARLES R. ANDREWS, Pastor of the Oak Lawn Baptist Church, Cranston, R. I.

The Committee included:

RAYMOND G. JONES,	Pastor of the Deep River Baptist Church, Deep River, Conn.
MERLE H. MASON,	Pastor of the First Baptist Church, New London, Conn.
CLYDE S. WOLF,	Pastor of the First Baptist Church, Brockton, Mass.

CONTENTS

INTRODUCTION

———◆●◆◆———

THE DEEP PROBING of the World Council Faith and Order
Commission and the intensive self-examination by member
churches are not unrelated. They find a meeting point in the
intensive questions of the age. Answers must be found to
urgent human questions. A common source underlies the
compulsion to understand the nature of the unity we seek
and the compulsion to re-examine the traditions of the distinctive churches. People who have not yet accustomed themselves to futility, meaninglessness, and death are asking the
questions: Where is hope when the horizons are obscured?
Where is unity when life has been fragmented? What is love
when calculated brutalities prepare to rain their bombs?
Where is God when meters gauge the atomic fall-out?

The quest for unity among the churches and the critical
examination of the traditions are not born of futility, however. They are born in a resurgence of faith. A vast confidence in God has led Christians to search for the answers

13

they believe may be found. The awareness that the status quo of the churches is not sufficient for the age has but deepened the urgency to find the basic answers. The search is for the redemptive power that broke forth through the death and resurrection of Christ. It is the Christian hope in an age of despair. In an age when improved material and human resources within the churches have not enabled the churches to penetrate the gathering gloom, men have turned to the Scriptures and to the church traditions believing they can find the clues to the redemptive power, the Christian hope.

It is true that there is no way by which Dietrich Bonhoeffer's [1] prison desk can be simulated, but it is equally true that living theology must be sought in a sensitive awareness of human needs. Even so, a vital theology cannot start "anew." It must build from the Scriptures; it must search through the traditions. In so doing, no doubt, like Bonhoeffer, the writers will move beyond the accustomed "positions" to seek new ground for viewing the richness of the gospel of Jesus Christ.

The search for a living theology is not a prerogative of the World Council of Churches or any one of the constituent communions. It is the responsibility of all Christian people. To the extent that Christians are aware of the shaking of the foundations, they will be driven to a re-evaluation of belief, polity, organization, and practice. It is imperative that questions be asked regarding the basis of our hope, the meaning of our corporate witness, and the motivation for service. In this sense the self-examination by churches can prove to be an "ecumenical" contribution. As a prerequisite to inter-

---

[1] Dietrich Bonhoeffer, executed by the Nazis in 1945 at the age of thirty-nine, not only left devotional writings (*Temptation, Life Together, The Cost of Discipleship, Letters from Prison*) but also had written substantial theological inquiries (*Communio Sanctorum, Akt und Sein, Schöpfung und Fall,* and *Ethics*). He wrote continuously from the Nazi prison prior to his death.

church communication and as a clarification of the meaning of the universal church, it can be considered ecumenical. It is assumed that a search for unity that does not seek for ultimate meanings will be fruitless. At the same time, it is considered idle to seek a unity when the constituent groups are unconscious of fundamentals. It is a working assumption that churches seeking an understanding of the realities of God are at the same time seeking the nature of the unity that should bind Christians.

In this setting American Baptists have launched a series of theological conferences. The first national theological conference ever held by American Baptists was called at Green Lake, Wisconsin, in 1954. It was preceded by two years of advance study-group preparation. Papers were prepared on a wide range of subjects:

> The Biblical Basis of the Gospel
> God's Design and Man's Disorder
> The Person and Work of Christ
> The Gospel and the Social and Political Order
> The Gospel and Man's Hope
> The Nature of the Church
> The Ministry of the Church
> The Government of the Church
> Baptism and the Lord's Supper
> The Church and the World

Members of the Planning Committee included Baptist delegates who had attended the Faith and Order meetings at Lund and who planned to attend the Evanston meeting of the World Council. It was natural that the conference at Green Lake should stimulate widespread discussion and engender unprecedented enthusiasm for theological studies. Sober evaluations, however, indicated that only surfaces had been scratched, and theological conversation had just begun. Clearly, American Baptists needed further studies. To continue the effort begun by the Green Lake Conference, the Planning Committee, under the leadership of chairman Wilbour E. Saunders, president of Colgate Rochester Divinity School, projected this second year phase. This resulted in five Regional Theological Conferences, held in the summer of 1956. The following subjects were assigned:

West Coast: The Christian Doctrine of God
West Central: The Christian Doctrine of Man
Middle Atlantic: The Doctrine of Sin and Redemption
New England: The Doctrine of Christ
East Central: The Doctrine of the Church

Because of the enthusiastic response to these regional conferences and the basic papers, a committee was charged with the responsibility of selecting seven papers for publication. The committee was composed of: Robert T. Handy, Robert G. Middleton, Robert G. Torbet, Winthrop S. Hudson, and Lynn Leavenworth, Chairman.

It was agreed that the selection, from among approximately 150 papers developed in the series of conferences, should reflect the range of inquiry, the direction of thought, and the level of competence which have characterized the theological studies. In principle, the committee proceeded to select at least one paper from each of the five areas of study assigned to the regional conferences. While relevance, freshness of insight, and readability were among the criteria, much priority was given to the relationship of one paper to another in the selection.

In addition to each paper selected for this volume, there were at least four papers prepared on other phases of the regional conference themes. Each of the present papers represents one of the aspects of a general theme. Of course, none of the particular papers was written in planned relationship to the other papers included in this selection. All seven of the papers in this volume bare these obvious limitations. Each writer, furthermore, has employed his own characteristic style of writing.

The purpose of this volume, then, is to gather seven essays, representative of the theological conference papers, to demonstrate the direction of thinking, to identify some of the problems of theological concern, and to provide material and stimulation for continuing discussions.

A further word of explanation may enhance the use of the papers. Each paper in itself is the product of group preparation and discussion. Although the writer in every case assumes personal responsibility for the handling of the materials and for the eventual form of the paper, each, nonetheless, sought to reflect the thinking of the group. As a writer he has served as the chairman-writer of a group of Baptists representing diverse backgrounds of viewpoint and profession. He was assigned the nearly impossible task of expressing his own insights while reflecting the viewpoints of the group.

It is obvious for the above reasons that the papers cannot be said to express an official denominational position on the given subject matters. They do represent what selected American Baptist scholars have had to say in preparation for conferences called by the American Baptist Convention for purposes of theological study.

Turning now to a consideration of the conversations as a whole, what can be said about their relationship to the total Christian concern for theological insight? In the first place, a genuine denominational humility has characterized the discussions. The studies appear to have been free from defensiveness. The younger men in the theological field, unlike their forerunners of a decade or two ago, appeared neither dogmatically to disavow nor uncritically to affirm their denominational heritage. In answer to the question, "What do we have to say to the wider Christian company?"

most of the American Baptists participating in these studies have been inclined to reply, "We, like other church bodies, must re-examine our own beliefs carefully and objectively understand ourselves and others." In this mood the search into the Baptist tradition appears to have its rightful setting in the total Christian communication.

In the second place, American Baptist scholarship reveals its dependence upon the broader base of ecumenical thought. Though it is imperative for Baptists to understand the central Christian affirmation, of course they do not entertain illusions regarding the possibility of a "Baptist doctrine" of God or of Christ as such. However, in the areas where Baptists have appeared to have a special traditional interest, the indebtedness to scholars from all church traditions is noticeable. In regard to Baptism and the Nature of the Church, Baptists have been helped by current thinking, for example, among Lutheran and Reformed groups. This, in itself, can be a weakness inasmuch as Baptists are not able to articulate their own tradition. The younger theologians especially have voiced a deep concern that the next phase of the theological studies center in a careful evaluation of historic materials related to the Baptist tradition. As one of them remarked, "We need to know who we really are, and understand the positions we have assumed as Baptists before we can think competently and creatively in the field."

In the third place, the eagerness with which Baptists respond to the theological studies undergirds the real hope of more adequate articulation of the Christian faith in the future. This concern for theological study has characterized most church groups in this decade. It is a sign of health and promise. There will be denominational strength and total Christian strength as competent theologians are developed and as students are led to explore the areas of traditional concern. For Baptists some of the areas demanding attention include: Regeneration, the Nature of the Church, Relationship of Church and Culture, the Ordinances, the Christian Vocation (laity and ministry), and the Principle of Individual Freedom and Responsibility. Such studies no doubt will prove relevant to the wider discussions concerning faith and order.

For Baptist ministers and laymen, these papers should help to identify some areas of much needed discussion. They should suggest other areas not covered in this volume. The setting of the problems and the direction of the answers should provide incentive for exploring the Baptist tradition within the setting of the current wider theological discussions. Even though these papers may not be understood as authoritative or even exemplary in themselves, they may commend themselves as resource material for individual reflection and group study.

For readers from the wider Christian family, these papers should indicate the approach that is made by one branch of the Christian family. The problems belong to all Christians. They are rooted in urgent human needs. These papers should be viewed as an intensive effort by Baptists to share in the Christian task of understanding the meaning of the faith we profess.

I

THE BIBLICAL BASIS OF THE GOSPEL

WALTER J. HARRELSON

THE BIBLE AND THE GOSPEL are inseparable, though not identical. The gospel is God's good news for all mankind—news of forgiveness of sin, victory over the powers of darkness and death, news declared to mankind in the ministry, suffering, death, resurrection, and promised return of Jesus Christ. But we see that the word "gospel" has a double meaning. On the one hand, the gospel is the news that certain *events* have in fact taken place—that God has established in Jesus Christ his kingdom. This is what God has done. On the other hand, the gospel is the *message* proclaiming these events. This message must be formulated in human language, capable of being communicated to others who understand the language. The gospel would be false if the events of which it speaks had not taken place. But the events would be meaningless *for me* if they were not told me.

The Bible tells of these events. In a sense, then, it *is* the gospel, in that it is the bearer of God's good news. But in a more important sense it *rests upon* the events. The gospel has its basis in the saving acts of God which are most fully

21

and adequately described in the Bible. The message of salvation could conceivably be declared in non-biblical language, but the entire history of the church makes it clear that this has seldom, if ever, taken place. God's good news in Jesus Christ rests upon deeds done and there is no more adequate description of these deeds than that which the Bible contains, and none at all that is not dependent upon the Bible as its source.

I. THE AUTHORITY OF THE BIBLE

The Bible has a unique place among Christians as the bearer of God's good news and as the critic of all formulations of that good news. It is the authoritative witness to the saving deeds of God among Israel and in Jesus Christ. The nature of the Bible's authority, however, is difficult to state because of the following considerations, among others: 1. The Bible is in some sense a document of the church. While the events of which the Bible speaks are prior to the church, the church nevertheless has produced the Bible in the form in which we have it. 2. The Bible requires the enlivening and empowering activity of the Holy Spirit in the church and in the life of the individual believer in order that it be received and comprehended as God's Word. 3. It is the risen and reigning Christ who has all authority in heaven and on earth (cf. Matt. 28:18), and thus our final authority as Christians is the living Christ, known through God's actions recorded in the Bible, under the guidance of the Holy Spirit in the fellowship of believers.

The authority of the Bible is frequently set forth in ways which limit the full range of its actual authority. The following are some of the ways in which the Bible's authority is inadequately stated.

1. For some Christians, the Bible as a written book has

been adopted as the *one* authority. The biblical words, preserved throughout the centuries on manuscript and on the printed page, are looked upon as God's own words to man. This means that the Bible and the gospel are not only considered inseparable; they are made identical. The deeds of God are made secondary to the words which describe the deeds. Such an exclusive reliance upon the biblical words can easily degenerate into the worship of the Bible itself, rather than the Lord of the Bible.

2. Other Christians have avoided the danger of worshiping the biblical words by selecting from within its pages certain leading ideas or principal teachings which are given authoritative standing, while the remainder is considered to be of lesser force and validity. While it is true that there are great themes and central teachings, if these are simply lifted out of the whole Bible and given a special status as normative, on what principle is such a selection made? One salutary guide in this process of selection is what Paul calls "the mind of Christ." If the authority of given biblical assertions is judged in the light of the mind of Christ, there is a usable criterion for determining what is central to the biblical witness. But it is obvious that such a view could lead to complete arbitrariness. Who knows in a given instance just what Jesus would have said or done in a contemporary situation? Who can say of himself with complete self-confidence, "I have the mind of Christ"?

3. Still other Christians have appealed to conscience or the "inner light" as the supreme religious authority. The Bible often receives a high secondary place of authority, but conscience—the individual or corporate conscience—is given the primary place. And again it is clear that this is a denial of the inseparable connection between the Bible and the gospel.

4. A most tempting solution to the question of the nature of the Bible's authority was proposed early in the life of the

church. On this view, the *church* is the primary preserver and interpreter of the gospel. The Bible has been preserved, and its limits have been fixed, by the church. God has conferred upon this institution the authority to interpret and to promulgate the gospel. The Bible is important, but only the church knows how to read it properly. The dangers of such a view are quite clear. Actually it means that the gospel and the church have been identified, and the inseparable connection between the gospel and the Bible is compromised.

A. *The Baptist Position on the Authority of the Bible*

The early creeds and confessions of Baptists demonstrate that the Bible was looked upon as of indubitable authority. The Confession of Faith of 1677 states that "Holy Scripture is the . . . infallible rule of all saving knowledge." [1] In the New Hampshire Confession of 1830 this is even clearer: "Scripture had God for its author . . . without any mixture of error." [2] This statement obviously approaches the notion of plenary inspiration.

Many of our greatest scholars and theologians have pointed out the central position which the Bible has occupied in Baptist thinking. H. Wheeler Robinson has observed that "constant appeal to Scripture . . . helped to make and keep Baptists a Bible-loving church." [3] And A. H. Newman has written as follows: "Baptists . . . are anxious to be instructed in the word of God . . . and are ready to abandon any position that can be shown to be out of harmony with apostolic precept. . . ." [4]

[1] From *Baptist Confessions of Faith*, p. 227, by W. J. McGlothlin; copyright 1911, by A. J. Rowland, Sec'y, American Baptist Publication Society, Philadelphia.

[2] *Ibid.*, p. 301.

[3] From *The Life and Faith of the Baptists*, p. 8, by H. Wheeler Robinson; Methuen and Co. Ltd., London, 1927.

[4] From *A History of the Baptist Churches in the United States*, p. 7, by A. H. Newman; Charles Scribner's Sons, New York, 1894.

Baptists have been generally in accord with the Reformation emphasis upon the centrality of Christ himself as supreme authority for Christians, with full recognition of the proper authority of the Bible, the church, and the Christian conscience. The Baptist insistence upon freedom from hierarchical control has led, however, to a certain modification of the Reformation emphasis. Our independency has been both a strength and a nemesis for us. Our emphasis upon *regenerate church membership* was the new contribution to the Reformation witness. Baptists emphasized that the Christian community must consist of those who had been "born again." For this reason there developed the practice of voting on the question of admitting new members to the church.

John Smyth carried this principle so far that he found it necessary to baptize himself. When later on he was troubled in mind about the seriousness of his action, and wished to return to a church with apostolic succession, his followers actually excommunicated him from the church which he had founded. In doing so, their authority was, as they believed, Christ himself, who alone could give validity to ordination or to baptism. The authority of the New Testament, therefore, particularly in its description of the nature of the redeemed community, was normative, but this authority was to be exercised under the guidance of the spirit of Christ operative in the Christian community.

One danger in the Baptist position, which was perhaps due to the insistence upon the normative character of the New Testament church, was that the New Testament might stand as authoritative to the exclusion of the authority of the Old Testament. It is well to remember that originally Baptists made little or no distinction between the Old and the New Testament as the Word of God.

The final position at which we arrive is the resolution

adopted by the American (then Northern) Baptist Convention at Grand Rapids on May 23, 1946.

> BE IT RESOLVED: That we reaffirm our faith in the New Testament as a divinely inspired record and therefore a trustworthy, authoritative and all-sufficient rule of our faith and practice. We rededicate ourselves to Jesus Christ as Lord and Savior and call our entire denomination to the common task of sharing the whole Gospel with the whole world.

B. *The Nature of the Authority of the Bible*

Baptists have not invariably held to a literal interpretation of biblical injunction. The Old Testament ceremonial regulations have not, of course, been binding, despite the fact that the Old Testament has been accepted as clearly authoritative, these regulations having found their fulfillment in the life and work of Christ. Nor were all the New Testament prescriptions and commands treated as binding—as, for example, saluting one another with a holy kiss (cf. Rom. 16:16) and anointing with oil (cf. James 5:14). Even a command attributed to Jesus himself, the washing of one another's feet (cf. John 13), has been taken literally by only a small group of Baptists while the intended principle of humility has been carefully preserved.

The Bible has been considered as authoritative but not always in a literal sense. Where the literal sense of a passage is clearly intended, it stands; in other cases, the context may indicate that a figurative or symbolic meaning is intended. E. Y. Mullins has pointed out that Jesus expressly rejected the view that all parts of the Bible are equally absolute and final.[5] And in A. H. Strong's *Systematic Theology* there are several similar statements. Note the following: "The Bible

---

[5] *The Christian Religion in its Doctrinal Expression*, p. 147, by E. Y. Mullins; Roger Williams Press, Philadelphia, 1917.

. . . presents to us divine truth in human forms. . . ." [6] "When the unity of the Scripture is fully recognized, the Bible, in spite of imperfections in matters non-essential to its religious purpose, furnishes a safe and sufficient guide to truth and salvation." [7] Baptists have in general been open to receive the results of all scholarship which has illumined the background and content of biblical faith. At the beginning of the modernist-fundamentalist controversy in 1922, John Roach Straton expressed this fact as follows:

> Whenever reverent and devout scholarship points to a better way through [the Bible's] sacred pages, we will gladly and gratefully follow. But as we look at it in the right way, we see shining through it the glorious and divine face of the Savior of the world. The shadows in the Book and its dim and obscure touches are an essential part of the total effect. And its authority is not arbitrary and artificial, but inspirational and vital.[8]

The Bible is the Word of God. This cannot mean, however, that the actual words of the entire Bible have simply been written by the finger of God. Behind the biblical story is the reality of Christ, his life, teaching, death and resurrection. The living Christ is our supreme authority. This fact, then, transforms the Bible from being simply a narrative of God's acts into the authoritative guide for life and practice. His commandments, the quality of his love and forgiveness, his invitation to the new life in God's kingdom—these are the foundations of all Christian living. The Bible then is authoritative because it reveals the fact and the truth of Christ, the incarnate Son of God.

We have a holy obligation to use the Scriptures as Jesus

---

[6] From *Systematic Theology*, p. 213, by A. H. Strong; copyright, 1907, The Judson Press, Philadelphia.

[7] Ibid., p. 218.

[8] Sermon preached in Calvary Baptist Church, New York City, published in *Calvary Pulpit*.

used them. In Luke 9:51-56 there is the account of James and John who wanted to call fire down from heaven on the Samaritans who were not willing to receive Jesus. James and John felt that they had good Old Testament precedent in the prophet Elijah (2 Kings 1:9-16). The response of Jesus was devastating: "You do not know what manner of spirit you are of; for the Son of Man came not to destroy men's lives but to save them" (Luke 9:55-56, RSV margin). Here Jesus went back to his fundamental conjunction of the moral righteousness of God at the heart of the universe over which no biblical precedent, however strong, or authority, however venerable, could ride, even if it were that of a Moses or an Elijah.

C. *The Canon and the Holy Spirit*

Finally, we must recognize the necessity for authoritative writings, if the church and the believer are to have any standards of faith and practice. The early church carried out a selective process in the formation of the canon. Its exact boundaries may be debatable, but some limits had to be fixed in order that the threat of heretical movements be met effectively. Even Martin Luther might call the Epistle of James a "right strawey" epistle; but the church has surely been led by the Spirit of God in its decisions that certain books tell the authentic story of God's saving deeds while others, however noble and helpful, are not essential to that story and may even state it in misleading or dangerous ways.

As Christians we are under solemn obligation to reject all rule of thumb, arbitrary, magical, and mechanical methods of interpreting the Bible. Instead, we must come to know that both the Old Testament and the New Testament, separately and together, can be rightly and helpfully understood only by interpreting what is written in the light of (1) careful examination of the precise meaning of the text; (2) the guidance of the Holy Spirit; (3) the corporate witness of the church across the centuries; and (4) our own growing experience as obedient followers of him who is both Light and Life. Here the triune God—Father, Son, and Holy Spirit—acts to reveal his Word, and his will, to initiate man's response, and to judge or confirm the character of that response.

II. THE UNITY OF THE BIBLE

A. *The Problem*

The Bible, as the name *biblia*—plural for "books"—suggests, is not a single, unified book at all. It is a collection of writings from many different periods, by a large number of authors, and with many differing points of emphasis. It is not a unity from the point of view either of authorship or composition. As a piece of the world's literature, it is more like a religious anthology. For the historian of the world's religions, it must be treated as a collection in a double sense: as a group of miscellaneous writings from the ancient Israelites, and as another group of equally miscellaneous writings from a new religious movement founded by Jesus of Nazareth and his followers. For the modern Jew it clearly represents two books, one sacred and authoritative, the other a noble collection of documents from an unorthodox Jewish-Christian sect.

When the Christian speaks of the unity of the Bible he must never deny that it is also a collection of very diverse documents. The work of literary and historical criticism, despite certain excesses, has been of invaluable service. The unity of which he speaks arises out of his conviction that the Old Testament and the New Testament together comprise the dramatic story of God's choice of a people, his covenant with them, his guidance and promises to them, and his mighty deeds of salvation which culminate in the gift of his Son for the world's salvation. The problem which is posed by the Christian's claim that the Bible is one book is this: what is the relationship between the Old Testament and the New?

At least two possible answers are available, both of which are reasonably satisfactory. The first is that the Old Testament and the New Testament together tell the story of God's salvation; the Bible is thus sacred history, the history of God's redemption of mankind. The second is that the New Testament gives a full picture of God's salvation of the world, but that the Jewish Scriptures (the Old Testament) are accepted by Christians who see that the Christ is also the fulfillment of the authentic hopes of the Jews. Both answers affirm that the Bible is one book, but the second claims that the Old Testament is not indispensable to the full comprehension of God's salvation in Jesus Christ. The Bible, in this latter view, is one book, but only by virtue of the Christian's (or church's) acceptance of the Old Testament as authoritative in the light of the New. Traditional Christianity seems always to have accepted one or the other of these answers, in some form.

B. *The Baptist Position*

It is extremely difficult, of course, to determine any clear position of Baptists on this question. The Baptist insistence upon the centrality of the New Testament revelation has led in recent years, however, to the acceptance of the second answer more often than the first, it is believed. Our church life is patterned upon the order and discipline of the New Testament community—or at least it is our aim that this be so. Therefore the New Testament has a kind of authority which the Old lacks. All sacramental forms and institutions are looked upon with suspicion, our one priest is Christ, our major ordinances are baptism and the Lord's Supper, both absent from the Old Testament. As a result, the Old Testament is accepted chiefly in those instances in which it speaks of the Christ. The Old Testament must therefore become a Christian book in order to find a central place in our preaching and church life.

C. *The Old Testament Is Incomplete Without the New*

Let us approach a clarification of this situation by stating that the Old Testament demands a New Testament for its completion. All Christians will, of course, accept this as obvious, but it is equally clear that no religious body has ever found the Old Testament, as sacred Scripture, complete and adequate for the faith. The Muslims have the Qur'an. The Jews also have the Talmud and other collections of tradition. The Old Testament, as a Book, has never stood alone. It is impossible to live by the Torah apart from supplementary "revelation," as history has demonstrated. Those Jewish sects (e.g., the Qaraites of the Medieval period) which attempted to live by Torah alone were never more than a dissident minority voice in Judaism.

The Old Testament contains abundant evidence of its incompleteness. All the major Old Testament themes point beyond themselves. The promise to Abraham is nowhere described as fulfilled. The covenant with Israel at Sinai is always being broken; this must be so until the new covenant is written on Israel's heart (cf. Jer. 31:31-34). The land of the promise is precariously held; in fact, it is far from being a land flowing with milk and honey. Justice and righteousness, faithfulness and mercy never become the actual foundations of Israel's life. The shoot from the stem of Jesse does not appear. The suffering servant has his prototypes, but no more.

Even the order and arrangement of the Hebrew Old Testament speak plainly of its incompleteness. The Old Testament, in the order in which it is presented in the Hebrew manuscripts, trails off into a rather miscellaneous collection of "writings." The story has a marvelous beginning, but it does not come to an end.

Another indication of the incompleteness of the Old Testament is visible in those writings marked by a deep and agonizing hunger for meaning and for full communion with God. Often the heavens seem to be closed over the heads of prophet and psalmist. The covenant, the promise, the certainty of God's victory at the end are not able to provide that assurance of victory here and now which is so characteristic of the New Testament writings. The mighty wrestlings with God never cease till the Son of God himself stills them. All this can perhaps be summarized by the statement that the Old Testament is the book of promise; the New tells of its fulfillment.

D. *The New Testament Is Incomplete Without the Old*

It is equally true to say that the New Testament demands the Old for its completion. The New Testament, as the record of God's salvation, requires for its full understanding the story begun in the Book of Genesis. How could we possibly understand what is meant by the Christ apart from the Old Testament picture of the promised Messiah (cf. Isa. 9:1-7; 11:1-9; Mic. 5:2-4; etc.)? How would we be able to deal with the New Covenant in Christ's blood without our Old Testament picture of the Old Covenant (cf. Ex. 24:3-8; Jer. 31:31-34)? What meaning would we find in the notion of the fulfillment of Scripture, of which the New Testament speaks so often, if we ignored the promise to the Israel of the Old Testament (cf. Gen. 12:1-3)?

The New Testament simply takes as its point of departure the great drama of Old Testament revelation. The election of Israel, the covenant, the judgments upon faithless Israel, the great affirmations of the righteousness, justice, holiness, and love of God are all presupposed. The depth of faith revealed in the Psalms is a heritage implicity adopted into the Christian community.

We need only to examine the preaching of the apostles, as the New Testament records it, to see that constant appeal is made to the Old Testament. And this is true even when the gospel is preached to Gentiles. To those who never knew the Old Testament, the gospel is presented as the completion of God's work begun with the fathers of old. Every New Testament book except the epistles of Philemon and John contains quotations from the Old Testament.[9]

Another equally important fact is that almost the entire theological vocabulary of the New Testament is Semitic and is hopeless jargon unless it is illuminated by a study of the Old Testament vocabulary. Such words as sin, righteousness, justice, salvation, faith, hope, and love are all key terms in the Old Testament. While it is true that many of these words take on new shades of meaning or entirely new meanings in the New Testament, none of them can be fully understood through a study of the New Testament Greek words alone.

Another fact which is often overlooked is that the Old Testament provides a picture of the life of faith which is worthy of comparison, but not identical, with that in the New. There is displayed in the Old Testament the full richness of the life of man under God. Man appears in all his sin and misery, with all his possibilities for good. Man is not the center of attention in the Old Testament, for it is God and not man who is being praised. Because of this detailed picture of the life of faith, the Old Testament is a safeguard

---

[9] See the list of numerous quotations given in Nestle's *Greek New Testament* (18th ed., Stuttgart, 1948) pp. 658-71.

against heresy. It is no accident that many Christian heresies have arisen among groups who ignored or openly discarded the Old Testament. Christian faith can never accept the Greek notion that the flesh is evil, so long as the Old Testament witness is preserved. Sentimentality is avoided in the church wherever the ruthless and uncompromising word of the Old Testament prophets is heard. The holy God will never be made into man's big brother while the picture of the Old Testament God of holiness is read and heeded.

It is clear then that on at least four counts the New Testament requires the Old for its completion. 1) The New Testament themes, such as redemption, covenant, Messiah, are taken from the Old, and appear in their wholeness only when the two Testaments are held firmly together. 2) The New Testament has made constant use of the Old in its preaching and teaching, even to Gentiles; therefore, the New Testament itself demonstrates the indispensability of the Old. 3) The theological vocabulary of the New Testament needs the elucidation of the Old Testament, since the great majority of its key words are Old Testament terms. 4) Biblical faith in its wholeness appears only when Old and New Testaments stand together to complement each other. The Old Testament, when rightly understood, often saves the church from heresy.

E. *Jesus Christ, the Giver and Guarantor of the Bible's Unity*

If it is granted that the Bible is one book, then it is necessary to find the precise point at which this unity is made clear. For the Christian it is Jesus Christ himself who is the center of the Bible and of the salvation-story which it tells. He and he alone makes the Bible one book and not two or several. The Bible can no longer be treated, as it has been by many scholars and theologians, as merely a record of man's growing knowledge of God. There is of course a process of development which can to some extent be traced, from the earliest Old Testament passages to the teachings of Jesus. But there are major themes in the Bible from beginning to end which must never be ignored.

The unifying themes cannot be adequately seen, however, under the scheme which makes the Old Testament the book of prophecy and New the book of fulfillment of prophecy. Much of the Old Testament literature has no prophecy of the Messiah at all. Must all these books or passages then be removed or passed over in silence? This is precisely what many Christians have invariably done. But such a procedure indicates that the reader has made himself lord of the Bible; he dictates the message which a passage must contain in order to be fully authoritative.

Christ indeed appears in the Old Testament, but not primarily as the prophesied one. The more genuine bond between the Old Testament and the New is not that of prophecy and fulfillment, but of *promise* and *fulfillment*. The Christ is the promised one in the Old Testament, and the Old Testament is accordingly, in every book, the book of the promise. Ecclesiastes is a genuine biblical book for the Christian not because it prophesies of Christ—which it does not do at all. It is Scripture because it tells how one man (and many others with him, no doubt) wishes to believe God's promise, but is near despair because this promise seems to be denied by everything around him. The Song of Songs has nothing to say of Christ, but it has much to tell of how the people of the promise gladly accept the joys of love and marriage, how they exult in all God's gracious gifts. And it is the Christ and no other who is the fulfillment of this promise. This story of transcendent importance for the Christian culminates in Christ's coming, his obedience unto death, his resurrection, and his promised return at the end-time.

F. *Conclusion*

The Bible is one book, then, because it tells one story—the story of God's holy and righteous love for his creation and his firm oath and promise to save. The story begins at the very creation and ends with the new creation at the end. And it comes to a crescendo of joy and life in the gift of God's own Son, the Word made flesh, for the sins of the world. This story is marred and made fragmentary by any attempt on man's part to select the "core" or the "principal teachings" from the Bible. For we are confident that the Spirit of God was at work in the process of selection and testing which has resulted in the presentation to the church of this one Book—the word of eternal life. The Baptist insistence upon the primacy of the New Testament is entirely proper. But the Bible has a complete story to tell, and no episode must be neglected or ignored.

III. THE WITNESS OF THE SPIRIT

A. *Introduction*

Our task in this section is to indicate the place of the Holy Spirit in confirming and making explicit the message of the Bible. The basic issue has been, and is today, the relationship between the Word and the Spirit. The Word of God is not to be made identical with the actual words of Scripture. The Word of God is that communication of the Living God to man which comes when the words of the Bible are given life and power through the activity of the Holy Spirit. It is the Spirit which guides the church and the believer into all truth (cf. John 16:13). We have stated above that the Bible is authoritative in that it presents Christ to us, the gift of God for the redemption of the world. It is the quickening presence of the Holy Spirit, in the church and in the heart of the believer, which enables us to recognize and to respond to this saving Gift of God.

B. *The Holy Spirit in Baptist Thinking*

Baptists have held, in general, to the classical trinitarian formula in their theology. In their confessions of faith this formula is often stated, but with little definition of the various functions of the persons of the Trinity. For example, the New Hampshire Confession states that the three persons in the unity of the Godhead are "executing distinct but harmonious offices in the great work of redemption." [10] There are also some connections made between the Word and the Spirit in the confessions. In one of these the church is defined as "a company of visible saints, called and separated from the world by the Word and Spirit of God, to the visible profession of the faith of the gospel." [11] Another of the confessions contains the following statement:

> The Lord Jesus collecteth out of the world to Himself, through the ministry of His Word by His Spirit, those that are given to Him by the Father, that they may walk before Him in all the ways of obedience, which He prescribeth to them in His Word.[12]

The role of the Spirit has continued to remain crucial in the right interpretation of the Scriptures for Baptists. This role can perhaps best be analyzed if we examine it under two aspects: *private* interpretation which every believer is summoned to make under the guidance of the Spirit; and *public* interpretation which is made in the preaching and teaching of the assembled Christian community.

---

[10] From "Articles of Faith, II. The True God," in *The New Directory for Baptist Churches*, p. 514, by E. T. Hiscox; The Judson Press, Philadelphia.

[11] Confession of faith made by seven Baptist Churches in London, 1643; Hiscox, *op. cit.*, p. 29.

[12] London Confession of 1689; Hiscox, *op. cit.*, p. 30.

C. *The Private Interpretation of Scripture*

We have always believed that the New Testament was not given by God to a priesthood, to be by them diluted, compounded, and adulterated, and then retailed by the pennyworth to the people; but, on the contrary, that the whole revelation in its totality, in all its abundance of blessing, with all its solemn warnings, and its exceeding great and precious promises, is a communication from God to every individual of the human race. It is given to the minister in no higher, or better, or different sense, than it is given to every one who reads it. Every one to whom it comes is bound to study it for himself, and govern his life by it.[13]

This quotation sharply defines the Baptist position on the right and duty of every believer to turn directly to the Bible for the disclosure of God's will. Every true believer is considered to have competency, under God, to discern through the Scriptures what is necessary for salvation. The famous doctrine of "soul competency" is to be understood as a repudiation of the necessity of any *earthly* authority in religion, not as a denial of the necessity of the work of the Spirit. Wayland makes this clear in the words which follow:

In our present condition of moral and intellectual darkness, we are incapable of knowing the things of God, unless the Spirit of God enlighten us. The presence of that Spirit has been promised to us whenever we seek it. . . . Relying on these promises, we may then ask in faith, nothing doubting, and confidently expect that the Spirit will lead us into all necessary truth.[14]

The issue which arises at this point is clear. There is no explicit distinction made between the action of the Holy Spirit in the life of the individual believer and the action of the Spirit in the church. No sharp distinction is necessary

---

[13] From *Notes on the Principles and Practices of Baptist Churches*, p. 132, by Francis Wayland; Sheldon, Blakeman, & Co., 1857.

[14] *Ibid.*, p. 303.

or even proper. But many today are greatly concerned about the dangers of private interpretation of the Bible which is not subjected to the common mind of the worshiping Christian fellowship. We shall return to this issue later on; just now let us examine the question of public interpretation of the Bible under the guidance of the Spirit.

D. *The Public Interpretation of Scripture*

Baptists have insisted upon a regenerate church membership in order that (among other things) the Spirit might freely function in the body of believers at worship and during instruction. For, as H. Wheeler Robinson has said, the church constitutes "the temple of the Holy Spirit in larger ways than the individual temple of a single life can offer." [15] This is not to reject the notion of a regenerate church membership, for in just such a congregation is it to be supposed that the Spirit would fall upon more fruitful soil.

> Baptists must and will continue to stand for the truth of a regenerated Church membership expressed in believers' baptism; but they will never make that testimony as effective as it ought to be till they have added to it a nobler Church-consciousness, and a profounder sense of the whole group, as well as of the individual life, as the arena of the Spirit's activity.[16]

In order that the free exercise of the Spirit might be safeguarded, all public worship in Baptist churches has been marked by the greatest freedom from set forms. Early in the Baptist movement this insistence upon "spiritual worship" was carried to such an extreme that even the reading of the Bible in the printed translations available was said to be "the invention of the man of sin, it being substituted for a

---

[15] H. Wheeler Robinson; *op. cit.*, p. 173.
[16] *Ibid.*, pp. 173-174.

part of spiritual worship." [17] There has always been a certain suspicion of written prayers, liturgical uses, and the reading of the sermon, since these might impede the free activity of the Spirit. In recent years there has been a movement toward a measure of formalism, liturgy, and carefully prepared prayers and sermons. While the dangers of formalism are not to be ignored, it is certain that the freedom of the Spirit is by no means compromised or restricted by the most careful preparation and attention to the proper forms of spiritual worship.

In the teaching of the church the Bible has been our textbook. Instruction has been aided, especially in recent years, by the use of a variety of other materials, but the end in view has constantly been the teaching of the message of the Bible. But these classroom sessions have always been set in the context of the Christian community at worship. The devotional focus, the use of hymns, prayers, and responsive readings have been consciously designed to prepare the minds of teacher and pupil alike for the coming of the Spirit, to bring life to the biblical word.

E. *The Spirit and the Word*

This action of the Holy Spirit in bringing life to the Word is absolutely indispensable, if the church is to accomplish its ministry of preaching and teaching. We have noted that the Word and the Spirit are closely linked in the Bible and are not to be separated. It is important to remember that the special domain of the Spirit is the community of faith. Therefore, while it is correct to insist that the Spirit quickens the heart of the individual believer in his prayers and study, the

---

[17] See the tercentenary paper by Principal Gould, "The Origins of the Modern Baptist Denomination" in *Transactions of the Baptist Historical Society,* Supplement to Vol. II, No. 3 (London: Baptist Union Publication Department, 1911), p. 204.

Spirit most particularly operates through the body of Christ, into which the Spirit has been breathed, to give it life and power.

How does the Spirit bring the biblical word to life and make it binding upon hearers and readers? This is a mystery which no one can fully fathom. But let us remember that in the Old Testament and in the New, the Spirit of God appears as the *empowering* agent in human life. When we speak of the Bible as inspired by God, we mean more than that God has guided the thoughts of the writers. The Spirit gives authority to the Word. By the Spirit we are made contemporaries with those who were the audience when the words were spoken. By the Spirit the words become bearers of the Word made flesh; they are suddenly transparent, and the glory of God streams through them. This experience is attested throughout the history of the church. There are no fixed times or circumstances in which this must take place. It is an experience of individuals, of family groups, but above all of the Christian community in its work and worship.

In this connection we can refer to our discussion of the authority of the Bible. There it was maintained that the Bible is authoritative because it presents Christ to us. This presentation is the work of the Holy Spirit in the life of the believer and the believing community. It is also the Spirit which enables us to grasp the unity of the Bible. The mind can discern the incompleteness of the Testaments when they are separated, but it is the Spirit of God which has led to their union in the early church and which reveals their unity in Christ.

The Spirit is thus seen to be the empowering agent which makes the words of Scripture vital and effective in the life of the individual and of the church. Although the Word becomes a channel of grace to the individual only as he yields to the work of the Holy Spirit in mediating it to him, the

Word is a standard of judgment for the individual whether he yields to it or not (cf. John 12:48). It is a proper corollary of this statement that the Spirit may become arbitrary power if it is separated from the words of Scripture. Private interpretation of the Bible must always be subjected to the testing of the Spirit, and this testing takes place in the regenerate Christian community, in the fullness of its worship and service (see 1 Cor. 12-14).

IV. FAITH AND REASON

A. *Introduction*

In the lives of all Christians there should be a place for both reason and faith, for both thinking and believing, for both understanding and trust. And while we may soon come to see that we can never fully understand all the deep things of our faith and surely can never adequately express them in human speech, we should nevertheless keep on trying to do so. We should go as far as we can in achieving both a reason for the faith that is in us and a satisfying statement of that faith, and should never be satisfied to live only in a mood of praise and devotion wholly divorced from wonder and search. We shall never in all our searching wander far from him who is our Lord if at all times we shall find ourselves "unafraid to reason and unashamed to believe."

The Bible, while not a textbook in the whole realm of knowledge, is nevertheless an infallible guide to God, under the illumination of the Holy Spirit and the witness of the corporate fellowship of the church. When in the past three centuries prevailing notions of infallibility were questioned by the advances of science and historical criticism, the Bible's authority suffered severe shock. Today we stand generally in the embarrassing position of declaring the authority of the Scriptures without being able to give sufficient substance to the term for it to have a compelling meaning. To some, such large sections of the biblical record seem to have been demolished by science, such as the story of Creation and the miracles, and other sections have been confused to such an extent by historical criticism, that the simple statement of authority is itself bewildering, and to a large degree seems like waving the flag long after the battle is lost.

In this historical situation faith and reason have been separated. Reason becomes associated with science and its modern disciplines, and faith is claimed all the more passionately by religion. In such a schism, reason is greatly reduced and identified only with its cognitive function, becoming largely *technical reason*. On the other hand, faith takes to itself the indubitable mysteries of revelation. In their extremes, then, reason becomes arrogant, assumes its own infallibility, and sets itself up as final judge of all validity. Equally extreme, faith becomes anti-intellectual, dogmatic in the worst sense, and assumes the role of an absolute judge. Thus separated, reason and faith are no longer able to approach the Scriptures hand in hand, but only as conflicting enemies.

B. *The Baptist Position*

In our Baptist tradition the variations of this perennial struggle may be seen. It would seem as if the fundamentalist position in accepting the Scriptures as literally inerrant was unmistakably on the side of faith. On the other hand, liberals and modernists by their discriminations and grading of the Scriptures were plainly on the side of reason. And yet this easy classification does not account for the extremely rigorous schematization of the Bible to which all fundamentalism is prone, and which is obviously the result of reason operating with its usual dogmatic absoluteness within the sphere of given data. In some ways the fundamentalist interpretation is much more rationalistic, though less historical, than the modernist. On the other hand, while the liberal position is obviously on the side of reason, yet faith is plainly expressed in the candid search for that which can be accepted completely by the modern man. Thus, any number of variants may be found.

Our Baptist tradition of freedom, criss-crossing with the authority of the New Testament, manifests this same dilemma. "Freedom" is a result of two quite different factors in the Baptist tradition: faith as it comes from our pietistic origins; and reason in its individualistic pretensons. And "authority" is a mixture of reason's demand for validity and faith's assumption of ultimate certainty.

C. *Our Present Task*

Our essential problem is to bring together these warring antagonists. Until faith and reason get together with some degree of unanimity, the authority of the Scriptures will be compromised and impoverished. Neither faith nor reason can fulfill their jobs alone. They need each other to support the total implications of authority and of revelation. Man cannot be truly redeemed unless the revelation speaks to every aspect of his being and releases all his energies in the unity and creative freedom of life.

But how shall this be done within the tradition of Christianity generally and more specifically within the context of Baptist principles? The first step is to discern that the *revelation* which gives the New Testament its peculiar authority for the life and destiny of man *is itself a union of faith and reason*. All the questions which reason had asked are satisfied by the revelation of Jesus Christ. There is no other way to clarify the power and freedom which came to the early Christians than by the assumption of an opening of a new dimension of life in which the old dilemmas of the law and sin were resolved. This was an access of reason, not apart from faith but in faith. Indeed, faith may be said to have given reason new perspectives by which it could move beyond its stalemate into the freedom of new worlds and new meanings hitherto unsuspected. Faith minus reason (Logos) becomes incommunicable and finally takes refuge in the esoteric and ecstatic. Reason minus faith becomes unredemptive, and finally culminates in lending to the demonically destructive evil the full resources of technics and civilization. This, however, is only the first step.

The second step regards the method of achieving in our own day such a union. This obviously is by far the more difficult. First, reason must be liberated from the reductions it has suffered at the hands of science to mere technical, analytical, and cognitive tasks—so-called scientific reason. Secondly, faith must be freed from its ecclesiastical and obscurantist restrictions. This implies a third necessity, namely the rethinking of revelation and the nature of man's unity in God. Both the Old and the New Testaments are salutary guides in this rediscovery of the true relationship of the whole man and God.

The theoretical path to the union of faith and reason is one most simply described as returning to the same depth of life, regardless of the accident of our historical era, wherein the revelation of God unites both faith and reason, where reason is fulfilled and faith is confirmed. It is as if we would only regain access to the authority of the New Testament in which the revelation speaks when we are willing to dig through the superficial surface formations that hide and cover the deeper stratum of such precious ore.

The practical problem is to recover the spiritual experience of the revelation in Christ, manifested in the New Testament and taken to be its authority. This experience neither antagonized the full scope of reason nor did it become the refuge of a blind faith. It would support authority in the sense of fulfilling reason in its largest sense and true magnitude, and of certifying faith with an ultimate center in which true reality was perfectly revealed. This would mean that the Baptist principles of scriptural authority could be declared with conviction as over against all subsidiary ecclesiasticisms or rationalistic literalisms. The authority is vested in the revelation; the revelation is not automatically operative without the complete consent of the person; by faith it is received. An inner grace, a gift of God, the authority itself, is in such a sense revealed, and not proved.

To be sure, this would mean that the creedal statements sufficient for a previous age, before the split of reason and faith became so wide, can scarcely serve as adequate guides for our own time. Here the Baptist rejection of "final" statements is to be respected. The spiritual dilemma of our time, developed by the scientific methodology and historical criticism of the last three centuries, demands that we again take upon ourselves the labor of interpreting the revelation in Christ Jesus in such terms that reason and faith may again be justified. Obviously this means a new and deeper exploration of the meaning of miracle and biblical saga, of the redemptive force in reality, of the nature of the incarnate Logos, and of the pertinence of the gospel for man's fulfillment.

V. AUTHORITY AND PLACE OF CREEDS AND CONFESSIONS

A. *The Foundational Creed*

Any discussion of the place of creeds and confessions must begin with the recognition that it is the New Testament in its entirety which is, in a special sense, the Creed [18] of the church. For the New Testament is the primary statement concerning the Christ who is the foundation-stone of the Church. It is the "rule and plumb-line of the church," [19] a "trustworthy, authoritative, and an all-sufficient rule of our faith and practice." [20]

The scope of this New Testament Creed is neither too narrow nor too wide. The New Testament is not, of course, to be taken as independent of the Old; it is rather the fulfillment and interpretation of the Old Testament. As the primary witness to God's self-disclosure in Christ, the New Testament is our all-sufficient summary declaration of Christian faith. Nor is this Creed too all-inclusive. We dare not limit the basic Creed even to certain statements from the New Testament itself, for such a procedure would impair the wholeness of this apostolic witness to the act of God in Christ. It would also open the way to arbitrary private interpretations of which aspects of God's salvation in Christ are central.

This Creed has characteristics which are found in no other creed. It is final, given in and with the Incarnation, coming out of the act of God which created the church. It is not so much created by the church as by the events which culminate in God's gift of his only Son. Further, as the living record of that event which created the church, the New Testament Creed constantly breathes creative life into the church. It carries on the event of which it speaks, through the action of the Holy Spirit, and in this way makes God's self-disclosure always contemporary with the ongoing life and witness of the church.

---

[18] Where the word 'Creed' is capitalized in our treatment, it refers to the New Testament.

[19] German Baptist Confession of 1834, art. X, W. J. McGlothlin; *op. cit.* All quotations from the historic creeds are from this work.

[20] Resolution of the Northern (now American) Baptist Convention, Grand Rapids, 1946.

B. *The Historic Creeds and Confessions*

It is clear from the New Testament itself that the Christian community has found it necessary in its preaching and teaching to formulate summary statements of this basic Creed.[21] Such statements are what we mean by creeds and confessions. The church has found it necessary to formulate such summary affirmations of the faith throughout the centuries. The intention of the church in every such instance has been to state what is, or what should be, held by the Church Universal. A creedal formulation intends to state the essential faith of the entire Church of Christ.[22]

Three major functions have been served by the historic creeds of the church. In the first place, the early creeds and confessions have been marked by an almost hymnic quality. They are often paeans of praise to God for his inexpressible gift, confessing that "Jesus Christ is Lord, to the glory of God the Father" (Phil. 2:11). This might be called the devotional or liturgical function of creeds and confessions which marks them as highly important elements of Christian worship. The second function is to proclaim to all the world the doctrine, the faith of the Christian community. Creeds and confessions are therefore banners of the faith.

A third function is to provide short and succinct definitions of the faith for the purpose of the instruction of new members and to enable the Christian fellowship to point to a summary way of describing what its faith actually is. This is the theological function of creeds and confessions, a function much needed in the life of the church today.

---

[21] Note, for example, the creedal statements of Phil. 2:5-11 and 1 Cor. 15:3-7.

[22] For this reason, essential agreements are to be emphasized and differences written in charity. An excellent example of this principle may be found in our Second London Confession of 1677, in the Address to the Reader and in the Appendix. W. J. McGlothlin, *op. cit.*

But creeds and confessions have also been used in a fourth way as instruments of coercion and proscription of belief. Our principal Baptist confessions have clearly been intended for the first-mentioned uses. Although few of the Reformation documents can be called hymnic in form, they were certainly written in theological praise to Almighty God. With Baptists in particular, the second and third purposes for writing creeds and confessions were the dominant ones. From the very first, Baptists denied the identification of themselves with the Anabaptists and other sectarian bodies on the fringe of the Christian movement. They were always forced to explain themselves. Therefore, their confessions throughout their early and formative period were

> published in love . . . (1) to inform those who have a desire to know what Religious Duties they (the Baptists) hold forth: (2) to undeceive those that are misinformed thereof; (3) to the end that said Congregations may in love, and the spirit of Meekness, be informed by any that conceive they walk amiss.[23]

Thus it is fair to say that the primary purpose for which Baptist confessions were written was proclamation and definition of faith, and not proscription of belief. It is apparent that Baptist use for the latter purpose is misuse. This misuse of our confessions is no doubt largely responsible for the well-known suspicion of creeds by both conservative and liberal Baptist bodies. Such suspicion has sometimes resulted in the abandonment of any creedal formulations whatever, which has been a serious loss to the Baptist tradition. Correctly understood as proclamation to a heathen world and as praise to God rendered by the faithful, confessions have had and should continue to have a vital place in the life of our

---

[23] General Baptist Confession of 1651. Note also the Second London Confession which was written because "it was judged necessary by us to joyn together in giving a testimony to the world." W. J. McGlothlin, *op. cit.*

denomination. Their role as *relatively* adequate means for the succinct *definition* of the faith is also to be gladly acknowledged.

But this can only be maintained if the following characteristics of all creeds and confessions are kept in mind. 1. They are provisional and not eternal, expressing the thought of the church concerning given situations. 2. They are secondary and are to be based upon the fundamental Scriptural Creed, since they are interpretations of that Creed to meet contemporary issues. 3. They are limited in scope, emphasizing those aspects of the Scripture necessary in view of the situation which they attempt to meet. They may not even express Christian belief in its fullness (as is true of the Apostles' Creed, which omits all mention of the atoning work of Christ). 4. They are definitely creations of the church, expressions of its witness—and they may even be false witnesses. They must therefore be tested at all times by the norm of Scripture, interpreted in the Spirit.

Nevertheless it is true that creeds and confessions do have a relative permanence. The spiritual situations to which the church speaks are usually about the same. The idolatries and self-assertions of men are tiresomely repetitious, and the salvation wrought by God in spite of them is amazingly constant. Therefore the continuing relevance of the creeds and confessions, whether ancient, reformation, or modern, to the continuing sin of men and nations, and the continuing adequacy of those statements of praise to God, is not surprising. This relative permanence of creeds should be admitted by Baptists more than is commonly done. It is in no way alien to our tradition to recognize this, for our forebears had high praise for the work of their Christian fathers.[24]

---

[24] In the Orthodox Creed of 1678, for example, the Apostles', Nicene, and Athanasian creeds are listed as "thoroughly to be received and believed." (Article 38) W. J. McGlothlin, *op. cit.*, p. 153.

Creeds and confessions may be called "church sermons." They are proclaimed on the basis of Scripture by churches or representatives of churches. Their authority, like that of any sermon, roots in the Scripture out of which they proceed, and in the inspiration of the Spirit by whose guidance they are written. They are to be on the one hand thankful hymns of faith offered to God, and on the other banners of God's salvation accomplished in Jesus Christ, held before the eyes of the unbelieving world. Their use as instruments of coercion is entirely illegitimate among Baptists.

C. *Unwritten Confessions*

There is a sense in which each denomination within the church proclaims by the very fact of its separate existence an unwritten confession and an aspect of the faith to which it witnesses with particular zeal. With us this is a regenerate church membership as witnessed to by believers' baptism. We stand for the element of personal faith as prerequisite to church membership, an element often lost by the church at large. The existence of our denomination is a confession—a witness to a portion of the faith which should be that of the Church Universal.

It must be added, however, that even this "confession" of our separate existence is not eternal. It may well be that as the ecumenical movement continues and develops, we might stand even more strongly for regenerate local church membership within the unity of the church than we do in our separate witness.

D. *Creeds and Confessions in Baptist Churches Today*

In recent years creeds and confessions have been used more as "clubs" than as banners of the faith. The result has been extremely serious. Baptists have become a people without a creed. Church covenants have frequently been documents so harmless and so lacking in theological content as to make it appear that Baptist churches were little more than fraternal associations. But a church without its banner of faith to present to the world, with no great hymn of praise to God upon its lips, is a church without the gospel.

Nevertheless, the existence of a true fellowship of faith must be prior to the formulation of a Baptist creed. The possession of the gospel itself is primary; the creed is but its outgrowth. The exciting fact of our time is that in the current revival of biblical and theological study, God's providence is now restoring to us the Christian witness which we had almost lost. The Spirit is again beginning to be evident among us. "Fundamentalist" and "modernist" are terms of little real importance today. A meeting place is being recovered—at the foot of the Cross. The simple fact that at this time we are engaged in this attempt to re-examine the theological basis of our Baptist position is a very significant sign of new life in this member of Christ's body. It may be that one of the effects of this renewal of the Baptist mind will be the drafting of a confession of faith suitable for our times.

But one thing is certain: such a confession is not to be an instrument for heresy-hunting. Creeds and confessions are intended for no such purpose. Our confessions must rather be a proclamation of our central Baptist faith, without frills or subtleties, designed for free and affirmative use by our churches.

BIBLIOGRAPHY

Cunliffe-Jones, Hubert, *The Authority of the Biblical Revelation*. London: J. Clarke & Co., 1945. 119 pp.

Hiscox, Edward T., *The New Directory for Baptist Churches*. Philadelphia: American Baptist Publication Society, 1928. 608 pp.

McGlothlin, William J., *Baptist Confessions of Faith*. Philadelphia: American Baptist Publication Society, 1911. 368 pp.

Mullins, Edgar Y., *The Christian Religion in its Doctrinal Expression*. Philadelphia: Roger Williams Press, 1917. 514 pp.

Newman, Albert H., *A History of the Baptist Churches in the United States*. New York: Charles Scribner's Sons, 1894. 513 pp.

Richardson, Alan and Schweitzer, Wolfgang, eds., *Biblical Authority for Today*. London: SCM Press, Ltd., 1951. 347 pp.

Robinson, Henry Wheeler, *The Life and Faith of the Baptists*. London: Methuen & Co. Ltd., 1927. 189 pp.

Wayland, Francis, *Notes on the Principles and Practices of Baptist Churches*. New York: Sheldon, Blakeman and Co., 1857. 336 pp.

II

GOD AND THE NATURAL ORDER

ROBERT B. HANNEN

THE GENERAL INTEREST of Christian thought is in the area of God and the personal order of being. The idea of salvation which is so central to all Christian theology and rightly commands the principal place in the discussion of Christianity is limited to humanity. The doctrine of God, however, has always been recognized to involve more than a relationship to persons. The whole realm of the non-personal cosmos, the vast fields of the natural sciences, is related to God as the source and sustainer of all reality.

Theology has not been concerned with the collection of data about the order of Nature, or with the analysis and classification of such knowledge, and theologians do not usually consider themselves competent to decide issues which are more properly the province of the physicist, astronomer, chemist, or biologist. It is inevitable, however, that if the doctrine of God is bound up with the meaning of the natural order, its origin, existence, and goal, the theologians are to that extent confronted with the task of investigating what the natural order is, and what type of relationship might subsist between God and Nature. It is difficult to say in abstraction what this will actually involve by way of knowledge of the sciences, but it certainly would seem to mean some knowledge of the scientific method and its conclusions. The theologian who talks about the natural order without having some acquaintance with the sciences and listening to what the sciences have to say is obviously exposing himself to embarrassment.

The Naturalistic Position

When the approach is made to the natural sciences it becomes very obvious that theological explanations of events are given no standing. The chemist, the nuclear physicist, the biologist, the geologist, and so forth, do not include divine agency in their explanations of events. The mathematical formula is the sufficient guide. These formulas range from the simple "H_2O" for water to "$E = mc^2$," the most comprehensive equation, which is Einstein's digest of the universe, and they all have the common factor of being both non-personal and non-theistic. This raises a serious question as to the necessity of any theological reference for the explanation of Nature. When this position is found in any form which denies the relevance of a personal Deity for the satisfactory explanation of events, the theory is known as naturalistic; i.e., an explanation in terms of natural forces. Naturalism would be this approach when it is erected into a total estimate of reality. Then Nature would be autonomous, a closed system, governed by necessity and positive law. It is a grim and disconcerting picture.

In this view, persons are the chance by-products of cosmic chemistry, and any values they believe in have an even less ephemeral status than their admirers. Even the sense of beauty in the sensible world of flora and fauna, the bird on the wing, the sunset over the hills, is a conspiracy to deceive by pretending that the world is something more than an extra large chemistry experiment. A poet can clothe it in the magic of words and make the physics laboratory of the universe look like a fairyland, or assert a naturalism which still uses the magic of words but produces James Thomson's *City of the Dreadful Night,* which describes the world as rolling "round forever like a mill" which "has no purpose, heart, or mind, or will." The basic reality is something called energy or radiation to which love and pity are unknown, and persons a mere fortuitous expression of the potential of Nature. This view eliminates God and every relationship between himself and man.

If this species of naturalism or postivism is true then Christianity is a product of imagination, at best a poetic and romantic way of describing an otherwise comfortless situation.

The Limitations of Scientific Method

There can be little doubt that the very spectacular successes of the sciences have given great impetus to this suggestion, and have sent religious editors on a frantic quest for some scientists who believe in God as well as in their professional activities. If the naturalistic pressure is to be really met, however, solid arguments will have to be produced to demonstrate the sectional nature of the mathematical interpretation, and the real status of the personal mode of being in ultimate reality. Without the reality of persons, for example, the mathematical formulae could not even be known. The limitations of the scientific method must be shown to be considerable and indeed to be of the first importance for any honest appraisal of the achievements of science.

The scientific method is at once the strength and the weakness of scientific research. It is its strength, because it

limits the area of research to what can be observed, and subject to controlled experiment. Given objects in space-time,
the scientist proceeds to analyze and classify, and may have
a practical purpose in mind, as in medicine and explosives.
It is its weakness, because it excludes from the inquiry what
cannot be treated by mathematics and explained in terms
of cause and effect. This, however, is the very area which
really matters in life for persons, the building of character,
the question of good and evil, of joy and sorrow, the meaning of life, love and laughter, the realm of values, and all
other personal experiences. These matters are not reducible
to formulae, and constitute a relatively unmanageable and
unpredictable element in reality. This fact cannot be over-
emphasized in an age that makes an idolatry of scientific
progress. Managing a home, falling in love, or pursuing
happiness by some scientific method is a certain road to frus-
tration, for mathematics is of little use in such matters. The
millenium is not necessarily one step nearer by all the in-
ventions and gadgets of the whole scientific and technological
panorama. This is not to say that the astonishing ability of
modern man to control the elements is a thing to be de-
plored. That would be a curious assertion, for in medicine
alone the benefits now possessed can only be received with
profound gratitude. What is being asserted, however, is quite
simple. It is that the meaning of life may not be either clarified or enhanced by an advance in technical skills. We are
born, we travel through our span of days, we die, and our
happiness depends more on our relation to persons than on
our possession of things. Life can be made easier in terms
of pleasure and pain by mechanical devices and medical discoveries, but it is not made more intelligible in any ultimate sense. Science can tell us how the physical world can
be manipulated, but not what it means. Once this is clearly
seen, the true values of life begin to reassert themselves.

If these values perish, then the awesome skills of the scientific wizard can be destructive of all, including the wizard and all his works.

God, Persons, and the Non-personal

The assumption that there are two fundamental kinds of reality, namely, persons and things, has been questioned by many. There are those who would prefer to say that reality as personal is the only ultimate. Others maintain that reality exists either in the form of a pluralistic or a monistic physical universe. Perhaps, it might be suggested, there is only God *or* the natural order, or that God *is* the natural order. Every possible combination and relationship has been suggested in the history of human thought, and to expound them all here would be tedious. The common-sense view on which life at a practical level is lived is that there is a real difference between persons and things. Persons are conscious, self-directing, and are capable of conceptional thought. Things are composed of physical elements which are devoid of these properties. Animals and other living beings come in between, in various stages of proximity to both extremes.

Traditional Christian thought has recognized these distinctions, and has asserted the superiority of the personal above the biological and physical. Within the personal, it has further asserted the distinction between God and human persons, and taught consistently that God is personal in a unique, complete, and uncreated way. The Bible is the source of this perspective, especially in its use of the categories of creativeness and transcendence. It is by the will of God that persons are brought into existence, yet never in such a way that they become gods, but only the servants of God. He alone is Sovereign, and as Sovereign he maintains a position which is forever closed to human persons.

Some Bible Attitudes

The great variety of places in the Bible which speak of the relationship between God and Nature can be reduced to a few types. There are, for example: 1. those that refer to the initial creative act as described in Genesis when God brought all the universe into being; 2. those that refer to his perpetual government of Nature, for instance, in his gift of the rain, the bounty of the harvest, and his knowledge of the death of a sparrow. "He who made the Pleiades and Orion, and turns deep darkness into the morning, and darkens the day into night, who calls for the waters of the sea, and pours them out upon the surface of the earth, the LORD is his name" (Amos 5:8); 3. those that refer to special events such as the incarnation and resurrection.

These relationships are more than the area of Divine power; they are also involved in his grace as the incarnation would imply. They involve a belief in transcendence, that God is "above" the world; but they require, in similar fashion, a belief in his ubiquity. Sometimes God is said to act directly and sometimes he uses intermediaries, such as his messengers, word, or Spirit. The general attitude to natural events, however, is that they are related to spiritual causes either good or evil, as if these spiritual forces were directly controlling all natural phenomena. The idea of natural law as a principle of explanation was not developed in biblical times and could not be expected in a pre-scientific situation. It is this absence of explanation in terms of universal law which marks the most obvious difference between the Bible and the modern world.

Things and Persons in Relationship

The relationship of God to human persons is full of enigmas largely issuing from the nature of space-time, but these difficulties are multiplied in any attempt to define the relationship between God and the non-personal natural order. In the personal order at least it could be assumed that God and other persons were of the same ontological status, but Nature seems to introduce a radical disparity when it operates according to principles of necessity, causality, and repetitiveness.

The traditional term to use for God in this connection is that of Creator. This posits an external relationship, that of the potter and the clay, with the potter creating the clay as well as shaping it, and taken to extremes it could end in Deism. Even if extremes are avoided and God is believed to be in some fashion present in his universe, then the various possible ways can be listed and a choice made as to which is the preferable explanation. Simple identification with the universe, for example, is not a live option, and occasional visitations to perform some special task seems to imply that God is subject to spatial limitations which would raise more problems than it would solve. Some kind of parallelism is the usual attitude whereby God is not a thing, but is always present with things and knows where things are and what is done by or to them. It is expressed metaphorically as light or air or sound which have a pervasive property in relation to other physical things. Sound waves can come through what appears to be a solid wall, and magnetism, light, energy, and other physical factors which can be expressed in wave mechanics have the strange property of doing what human persons cannot do. The most common analogy to the operation of God would be along such lines.

The analogy is weak, of course, in that wave mechanics permeation through other physical objects can be demonstrated, but persons cannot project themselves through physical objects in the same way. To say then, that all our experience is against thinking of persons as one thinks of physical waves, and in the next breath to affirm that we can think of God like that, seems to be in contradiction to the nature of God as personal. Perhaps it is best to acknowledge the weakness of the analogy while still affirming the omnipresence of Deity, and frankly to confess that no analogy can be adequate to describe what is by definition a unique situation.

Again, the idea that "In him we live and move and have our being" will raise such questions as, "Is God in touch with a bad man as much as a good man?" or worse, "Is he as much in touch with a stone as he is with a man?" "Is the Lord in the earthquake and the fire?" It becomes obvious that when the general idea of God as Creator and Sustainer of the universe is developed to the point of particular applications of it in this and that object, then the question becomes as bewildering as the difficulty of answering a child's naive questions about things around him. The usual answer of the Christian teacher is to say that God is where goodness, beauty, and truth, and where faith, hope, and love, are to be found. He is not where their opposites are in control, and furthermore, the proof that he is not there is the very fact that disvalues are regnant. It may be misleading then to say that God is everywhere, but more correct to say that he is wherever love is; misleading to say that he is all-powerful, but more exact to affirm that he is sovereign in all that he wills to do. There will always be a real perplexity in any idea of the immanence if the personal nature of God is to be sustained. Perhaps Aquinas has stated the best practical description when he argued that, while God is in everything, his presence is not of the essence or the accident of his creation. Rather the relationship is like that between an agent and that upon which it operates. This preserves the idea of God as working everywhere in providence, and as continually creative rather than static. This dynamic factor in the idea of God is especially prominent in modern theology and marks a real gain.

Six Areas of Debate

Several specific areas may now be selected for special comment. They will serve as samples of the range of discussion involved in the subject, and draw attention to issues that deserve the consideration of every serious Christian mind. The area is admittedly difficult. Neat and tidy answers are not to be expected to the questions raised, but nobody is going to be fooled by such answers anyway. The big issues of theology and philosophy are usually longstanding problems, and if simple answers were possible they would have been found centuries ago.

1. *Physical Sciences.* Voices have been raised from within the physical sciences to support the idea of God. One of Einstein's last essays was devoted to the question of the reality of God as the principle of order and energy in the universe, and the impossibility of thinking of God in terms of personality. The Deity has been defined as the aggregate of positive laws, as First Cause, the Supreme Artificer, and the like. Sir James Jeans in *The Mysterious Universe* spoke in high praise of God as the Supreme Mathematician. In some quarters it is now popular to identify God with Creative Process, the Immanent Agency, or the Life-Force. There is something in all this, however, which looks very much like borrowing of religious language to name what is not an object of religious worship. The traditional terms are retained to express a natural piety, when the traditional Subject associated with the terms is bowed out of the universe, or thought about in an untraditional way. If the physical sciences operate at a positivistic level the idea of God is irrelevant to their operations. By this God is not disproved. He is simply ignored, and rightly so, for the aims of science are quite

distinct from the interests of theology and philosophy. Scientists should not be expected to discover God some day at the end of a super-telescope or among the whirling mass of electrons, protons, neutrons, mesons, anti-protons, and so on, that share the fabulous interior of a bevatron. Far from being surprised that scientists have not found God, we should be thrown into consternation if they should say they had. In that case, we should be compelled to show the scientists their error.

2. *Biological Sciences.* The relation of God to the world of animal nature has never received the attention that it might deserve. The brute creation was outside the realm of salvation and hence was ignored in creed and tome. Nevertheless, many questions are being asked in the contemporary world about the continuity of all living things, the suffering and death in the animal world, and the nature of vital processes. Birth, pain, disease, and death were experienced before man appeared on earth, and many forms of life, organic and biological, have not survived. Why they appeared at all, or why myriad forms of life still continue to perpetuate themselves, is a question without an answer. Creation appears not as an act, but as a process showing much of the trial and error method of advance. Any idea that God made all the items in the animal world as a model maker designs and constructs his products and then infused them with a life principle is not convincing, and bears no relation to the long struggle of living things for survival.

On the other hand, the designs and patterns so obvious to the observer in ten thousand items in Nature seem to defy any source in mere random variations. Every blade of grass, every spider's web, every ant hill, is a source of astonishment and is far more marvelous than the finest human artifact. Of course, this astonishment is directed to the ingenuity and design of natural items, and not to the approval or disapproval of the apparent purpose which they serve. Illustrations abound of ingenuity which seems to serve cruelty of a diabolical quality. Biological observations do not all lead to admiration of what is seen, but often to grief that the utterly callous should so often appear. If there is an immanent teleology, a good purpose behind all Nature, it is a principle of faith and not of sight. Design in Nature may prove that God is clever, but not that he is good. The idea of the goodness of God has another source.

3. *Miracle.* Any discussion of the relationship between God and Nature involves consideration of the subject of miracles. The idea of special divine activity is common in the history of religion and is by no means confined to Christianity. Sometimes the Deity is thought to visit the world of men occasionally and each visit would be a miraculous event, but where religion leaves its more superstitious stages behind and a more thoughtful attitude is taken to natural events, the relationship between the divine and the mundane is divided into what is normal and what is abnormal. The miraculous is the sphere of the extraordinary. It is the way by which what is unusual is designated.

It is notoriously difficult to define miracle for the simple reason that it would not be miracle if it could be understood. The use of the term denotes a failure to comprehend what has taken place and a desire to assign its origin to a divine action. This is the general attitude, for example, in the Bible. It does not necessarily imply any theory of a breach or suspension of the laws of nature, for such laws are of much later formulation than Bible times. The several biblical terms for miracle describe a source of wonder, a display of power, or a sign or message.

It would be an anachronism to read our modern scientific theories into the non-scientific attitudes of the ancient world. In Bible times men thought of the world around them as inhabited by spirits, some good, some bad, who were always operating, and the modern approach by means of natural law was almost unknown. Evidence of divine power was expected and believed to happen in association with natural events like the Exodus and in support of individual prophets. All the peoples of Bible lands possessed endless stores of tales about the divine operations.

That there were miracles ascribed to Jesus was not a novelty. Paul also claimed to work miracles (cf. Rom. 15:18f.; 2 Cor. 12:12), and others are credited with wonder-working ability in both Testaments. Where God was present such things were expected. What actually happened in terms of scientific fact no one ever discussed. When the matter of what actually happened is raised there are only a few alternatives. Either a miracle is a divine intervention involving a breach or suspension of normal natural order, it is an acceleration of natural processes, or it is an abnormal natural event whose explanation is not known, and may or may not involve something contrary to established physical law. Whatever may be the explanation, and it need not be only one type of event that is involved, any belief in God as interested in man will lead to belief in the possibility of extraordinary events expressive of the Divine Will. To rule out God's ability to act in his universe except in terms of the regular sequences of events, to make him helpless in the toils of inviolable law, is to deny his existence as a person and define him in terms of mechanical process. A God who does not act, or who acts only by natural law, is another name for Nature.

Even if this be granted, however, there is another matter to consider. Every event which is claimed to be a miracle is not necessarily so. A claim does not validate itself. Supporting evidence that the claim is well founded and might be true has to be furnished and scrutinized, for literature is full of claims which are without evidence to substantiate them. This is the famous point of David Hume, that the veracity and character of the witnesses, and the reliability of the transmission, are all open to examination. Any court of law will illustrate the difficulty of evaluating evidence, and the same consideration applies to any claim that some particular event actually happened and was not explicable in any other than miraculous terms.

Again, a close watch must be kept on the loose use of the term "miracle" for any marvelous happening. In its Christian usage it means an event which God is believed to have created in order to express his will and convey a message. There is no difficulty in finding marvelous events. Indeed, it is difficult to mention anything in the universe which is not astonishing when it is closely examined. The smallest particle of matter is a source of more marvels and mysteries than the seven wonders of the ancient world. But that does not constitute an atom as miraculous. It is only put in that category when it is believed to be a special event generated by God for the conveyance of a message, which is in harmony with the nature of God. Hence a miracle is linked to faith. Only he who can see the meaning of the event knows the fact of the miracle. It exists for the eyes of faith. Otherwise it is just another event, the explanation of which is still obscured in mystery.

4. *Prayer.* The use that is made of prayer in Christian life involves the relation of the Divine to Nature. Sometimes the awkward questions are evaded in advance by defining prayer in terms of human adjustment to the Divine Will, but this limitation is not recognized in any standard collection of prayers. There is more to prayer than conforming ourselves to the will of God, or schooling ourselves in resignation to accept the inevitable with equanimity. Whatever difficult problems it may pose, a frank recognition of the

petitionary element in prayer must be given, as well as the facts of confession, adoration, thanksgiving, and obedience. In essence, prayer is communion with God and can be silent or audible, in speech or song, private or public, read or spoken without preparation, formal or ejaculatory. It is the sincere lifting of the heart to God.

The element of request and intercession is the most troublesome to the apologist. What does it mean to ask God to control the weather, to bring evil doers to confusion, to prosper a business enterprise, to protect our nation, to cure the sick, and safeguard the traveler? Multitudes are offering such petitions every day and the natural order cannot be arranged to suit every petition. There would be no natural order if all the requests were granted. It would disintegrate into ten thousand sectional operations in answer to specific requests of as many petitioners.

Again, to note another obvious difficulty, what is to be said of prayers which are apparently unanswered? There is a factor of selectivity in the divine actions which seems hard to explain. The most deserving are not always healed or helped, and the most saintly are not thereby given any preference. Nor does quantity of petition seem to make an answer any more potent or speedy than an ejaculatory request in a moment of emergency. Too often we believe we can discern the hand of God in a situation for which we did not pray at all, for we had no knowledge that the danger was present!

Again, if God knows our need better than we know it ourselves, what function does petition play anyway? Are we telling God what he does not know, or trying to persuade him to change from what in his perfect Wisdom he has decided to do? The attribute of omniscience seems to constitute a puzzle when related to petition. If God knows all and because of his concern will act with a perfect response to our need, then petition would seem to be not only superfluous but a reflection on the divine knowledge and love which passes all human understanding.

Such would be the argument of an intelligent inquirer, and yet this has never been a satisfactory position for the religious mind. The argument really says too much, for if God were wise, good, and all powerful and could operate as suggested, then the need which evokes his action could never have arisen. Indeed, the whole course of history would never have happened, for nothing short of perfection in every part of the universe would be possible. Any possibility of change therefrom would have been anticipated, prevented, and hence never have happened. Against what appears to be the logic of the situation, it is necessary to place the facts of religious experience; namely, that God is thought of as Love, as Divine Concern for the good of his people, and man stands constantly in need of his help. There may be problems in plenty in this description, but it offers something better than a theory which would make human history impossible. Prayer as petition is a response to belief in God's ability, and when it is accompanied by a sincere deference to his wisdom and motivation which is not self-centered, then the whole of Christian history and experience is testimony of its justification.

Perhaps the best analogy is the simplest one of a family situation where the children have many requests. The parents do not always explain why one request is granted and not another. There may be good and sufficient reasons, but they cannot always be communicated, and the children may get the impression that responses are made on an arbitrary basis. Perhaps the parents could have anticipated many requests; and perhaps many needs are met before or without the requests, but it does serve the needs of self-expression and development of character to encourage responsibility, appreciation of need, thoughtfulness, and an awareness of the work of the parents in the home. In some such way, the petitionary prayer may be understood as an essential item in communion with the Divine.

5. *The Mind-Body Nexus.* To relate God to the natural order is thus seen to be a hazardous venture. When Christian faith has formed the idea of God as supremely personal, the very quality of God's essence magnifies the problem, for it makes the difference between God and things all the greater. The same is true in ratio to the value put on human personality. How is it related to the corporeal body in such a manner that the unity of the person is sustained? If the self is given an impermanent status, wholly dependent on its biological base, then the problem of the body-mind relationship is simplified. But if a high value is set on personality, and the self is superior to the corporeal and capable of continuing in separation from the physical body, then the difficulty of describing the relationship is correspondingly increased.

It is reasonable to suggest that the question of God and the natural order may be studied in convenient compass by means of this more localized issue, for the ontological problem is much the same.

There are many classic studies on this theme. In contemporary research they are usually found in work related to genetics, endocrinology, and neurophysiology, particularly in current analyses of the functions of the brain. It is now beyond all dispute that physiological states deeply affect mental states and many precise correlations have been traced. The presence of certain chemicals in the body above or below basic needs may produce profound changes in disposition. The deliberate introduction of specific material can excite or calm a patient as is necessary in medical practice. It is now believed that the human brain operates by neuronal energy discharges which can be recorded, which means that the case for a soul or self of a spiritual as distinct from a physical nature is being made increasingly difficult to defend.

The construction of a case for a self as distinct from a brain is one of the outstanding and urgent demands of the present time, if the religious reading of the matter is to survive. The traditional line of approach is under heavy fire, and it is certain that if the distinction between soul and body cannot be sustained, that of God and Nature will not be either.

When the full argument is drafted it will probably demand that the whole question of the nature of the non-personal type of existence be examined as a possible source of as many mysteries as those associated with the personal. It cannot be allowed that to explain a thing in terms of energy is to banish all difficulty. Analysis is not necessarily explanation. It may only increase the need for it.

And, again, it will probably be found that knowledge of physiological processes must itself be real, if not more real, than the object of knowledge. Cognition cannot be expected to prove its own unreality. Its status in reality must be presupposed before even an argument about it can be begun. Hence, the knowing self must be as real as the thing which it knows. It may be more; it can never be less. In some such way it is possible to see the lines of an effective argument against the reduction of the self to a non-personal energy coagulation, although the relationship between what we call the soul and the body may remain baffling.

6. *Immensity as a Problem.* It is well nigh impossible to think at the level of the macroscopic and argue in terms of astrophysics. The mind reels at the immensities of space where measurements are in light years with light traveling at 186,000 miles per second. There is nothing very comforting in the fact that the nebula of which the sun is a member contains something between fifty and a hundred

thousand million stars, and, if that is not impressive enough, then the fact that there are some hundred million extra-galactic nebulae within the observable universe certainly is. How much more there is, nobody has the slightest idea, or any astonishment left to appreciate the information were it available. The cosmic spectacle destroys complacency. Nevertheless such an approach does impress the mind indelibly with what can be so easily underestimated, namely, that any question involving God has immense ramifications. It is never possible to speak of God in overly familiar, sentimental, and petty terms after a serious attempt to relate him to the vastness of Nature, the apparently illimitable depths of space-time. The size and age of the physical universe is so crushing that it is difficult to think of it at all. The mind is too numb with the devastating impact of sheer immensity. Kant may have been moved to awe by the majesty of the starry heavens above, but it may be surmised the more common reaction is one of terror.

If religion were simply a matter of emotion, then it would collapse in the face of the gigantic scale of the cosmos. It is only when we think our way out of the emotion of apprehensiveness that a recovery of perspective is possible. What does this logic of size amount to? Does the fact of physical bigness determine importance? The answer must be in the negative, and we must resist the attempt to bully and cow us to terror. All efforts to use space-time as a measurement of spirit are wrong in principle, for it is a matter of debate among philosophers as to the nature of the space-time continuum, and whether it is itself dependent on the knowing mind. Even if it were to be granted that the external world is in fact infinite, it would not affect the reality of personal values. Physical measurements and spiritual values cannot be compared, for they do not belong to the same mode of being. Certainly God is not to be estimated by the yardsticks of astrophysics, for the question is not, "How big is God?" but "What is his nature?" Data gathered from the study of Nature help very little in discovering the Object of religious worship.

There is considerable truth in the contention of Barth that all that man can find will be an idol, and it will seldom evoke the sentiment of reverence. All that can be constructed of God from scientific observation will be within the scientific world of space-time, governed by necessity and an object of scientific curiosity to be proved or disproved as the evidence fluctuates from decade to decade.

In brief, therefore, four points may be posited in relief of the terror produced by the immeasurable vastness of star-thronged space. The first is that it affects us in this way because we think of the universe relative to the size of our bodies. Measured by the furniture of earth, it is indisputably crushing. Choose this standard and the result is a foregone conclusion. An old poetic line phrases it, "What is it all but the murmur of gnats in the gleam of a million, million suns?" But this is only one of the many possible standards, and it is pure assumption to believe that it is the most important.

Secondly, the whole question of the nature of the physical universe is a debatable matter, particularly on the philosophical question of what reality would be like apart from apprehension by the senses. This is a center of furious debate and no final answer seems possible. In regard to knowledge, it is agreed by many, however, that what is known is inevitably affected by the nature of the recipient. What is seen by the human senses is deeply influenced, and to some extent constituted, by the nature of the receiving apparatus. Animals see, hear, and smell things that the human senses cannot know. There are waves in the air around us carrying music and speech which we do not hear, unless we have an instrument to convert them to our range of hearing. It is impossible even to imagine what a facet of reality would be like which was forever removed from the possibility of our ever knowing its existence because it moves with too great speed, is too small, or is otherwise outside the very restricted limits of our receiving station range. How much of space-time is simply relative to our type of receiving station is probably a question that will never be solved.

Thirdly, the major field of attention in contemporary research is the submicroscopic, rather than the immense. We stand in terror of the unimaginably small, whatever we feel about the huge. In relation to the atom, man is impressibly vast, but it is obvious immediately that this matter of size is not too important, for the smallest particle of the physical universe or the microscopic virus can be devastating.

Fourthly, it may be asserted with vigor that even though man is small compared with the immense, that does not make him less real. The facts of knowledge, conscience, will, love, and all the personal factors of life are not one whit less factual because of a question of the size of our bodies. If knowledge itself is said to be insignificant, then the knowledge of immensity as a sample of knowledge is also unimportant. The significance of knowing is always more certain, primary, and stubbornly real than the thing known. When this is firmly grasped and resolutely pressed in the space-time situation, the perspective is corrected. The observer can never be obliterated by the thing observed, where the appearance of the thing observed is dependent on the nature of the observer.

What the universe is as known to God is forever unknowable by us. We only know it as it is experienced by human minds, and assume that there may be some similarities in relationship. What the natural order is for us is what God makes possible for us to know by our five senses. Apart from these five senses we do not know what the physical universe is like, for we have five avenues of approach and no more. If we know anything of the physical universe, it is sentient knowledge, and by necessity, this kind of knowledge can only be possessed by embodied persons. Therefore, we know indubitably that we are related to the natural order through these five media, but cannot believe that God is so related unless we posit the five senses in him, which is absurd. It follows that whatever God knows of the universe, it is not our sentient kind of knowledge. What he knows is as the Supreme Spirit would know, and that is quite beyond our ability to fathom. Therefore we say that the universe may be far more than we are able to know by our limited organs and whatever more it is, is known to God. He is the Creator and Original Source of all that has being. His ways are not necessarily, if ever, our ways, and his relationship to what we call the universe is not always open to our scrutiny except as we believe we see his special presence in time and space by the historical events which have made possible the salvation story of the Christian gospel, such as the incarnation and resurrection.

BIBLIOGRAPHY

Baillie, John, *Natural Science and the Spiritual Life.* London: Oxford University Press, 1951. 43 p.

Dampier, William C., *A History of Science in its Relations with Philosophy and Religion.* New York: The Macmillan Company, 1929. 514 p.

Heim, Karl, *Christian Faith and Natural Science.* London: SCM Press, 1953. 256 p.

Mascall, Eric L., *Christian Theology and Natural Science.* London: Longmans, Green & Co., 1956.

Raven, Charles E., *Natural Religion and Christian Theology,* Cambridge University Press, 1953. 2 vols.

Rust, Eric C., *Nature and Man in Biblical Thought.* London: Lutterworth Press, 1953. 318 p.

Whitehead, Alfred N., *Science and the Modern World.* New York: The Macmillan Company, 1927. 304 p.

III

THE ETERNAL SON AND THE
INCARNATE WORD

VICTOR F. SCALISE

TODAY MODERN THEOLOGY speaks through a resurgent interest in Christology. The dialectic, the debate, the
changing forms of theological speculation have come full
circle to the central fact of the incarnation. "God was in
Christ reconciling the world to himself." On this rock
modern theology builds its structure of thought. The mood
and temper of the new theological orientation stems from a
fresh approach to the study of the New Testament and a
revaluation of classical Christian theology, as seen in the
writings of Søren Kierkegaard, Karl Barth, Emil Brunner,
Reinhold Niebuhr, and Paul Tillich, to mention only a few.
Gone are the theologies that sought in vain to justify religious convictions without adequate structures of faith;
gone are humanistic speculations divorced from the nature
and character of reality; gone is the fear stemming from
critical and historical radicalism. Today theology is a David
challenging the Goliath of naturalism, communism, secular-

ism, and forms of existentialism that end in futility and despair. A new dimension has been added to modern theology through its struggles with relativism; the new context of the tragic world has given it momentous power through fresh insights. Today modern theology is poised astride our secular culture, slowly regaining its former influence and power.

I. STATING THE PROBLEM

The central fact of the Christian faith is that God is redemptive love. It is in the incarnation that love stands revealed. The thesis of the New Testament is that "the Word became flesh." The doctrine of the person of Christ is rooted and grounded in the underlying assumption that Christ is the pre-existent Son of God; the image of the invisible God;

> for in him all things were created, in heaven and on earth, visible and invisible . . . all things were created through him, and for him. . . . that in everything he might be pre-eminent. For in him all the fullness of God was pleased to dwell (Col. 1:16-19).

The incarnation is the central fact of the Christian faith. God incarnated himself in Christ that through Christ he might achieve our personal and cosmic redemption.

The great paradox of the God-man is the peculiar original fact of the Christian faith. The divinity and the humanity of Jesus are held together in an indissoluble bond born of faith and attested by experience. The portrait of Jesus in the New Testament is that of a distinctly human being. He healed the sick, fed the hungry, cared for the needy, forgave the sinner, found the lost. He was born of a woman, poor, persecuted, hungered, tired; he was betrayed, crucified, and died on the cross. No attempt is made in the New Testament to soften or minimize these facts. Alongside this essential human portrait there is the awesome fact that Jesus is the revelation of God; the Word made flesh. "In him was life, and the life was the light of men" (John 1:4). After the tremendous transforming experience of the resurrection, the humanity and the divinity of Jesus fused into a pattern in the minds of the disciples and they saw him as the Lord of Glory.

The incarnation is the profound truth that God is not alien to his creation. Here we find the clue to the nature and character of God and a proper understanding of the meaning and purpose of history.

1. *The Jesus of History and the Christ of Faith*

Luke, the Greek physician, opens his story of Jesus with a series of vivid episodes, some poetic, some bold in character, but all throbbing with a latent note of tragedy. Among others a scene is given depicting an old saint, Simeon, holding the infant Jesus in his arms and declaring, "This child is set for the fall and rising of many . . ."(Luke 2:34). Simeon represents the old; Jesus, the new. But by selecting this symbolic episode, Luke gives expression to a sense of bafflement with which already in the first century the person of Jesus was viewed.

This sense of wonder and bafflement has not vanished with the years. The enigma of his personality is still a challenge. Men have sought to understand him, their search at times assuming the form of a careful investigation of the historical sources, at other times resorting to the gift of faith with which to pierce the veil of mystery.

For more than half a century the quest has been the historical Jesus. To discover his humanity was the distinctively characteristic element of modern theology. This gave a fuller understanding of the Gospels. But now the mood has changed and the present-day theology seeks to go further.

The school of thought known as Form Criticism contends

that the Gospel stories are limited as historical sources and consequently the historical Jesus cannot be captured; hence the Christ of faith takes precedence over the Jesus of history.

The historical movement, however, has left its legacy, and no present day theological school dares to reject the full humanity of Jesus. Form Criticism seeks to discover the essential message of the early Christian church, the *kerygma,* behind the distinguishable forms in the fragments that, according to their thought, make up the Gospel stories. They still accept Jesus, the human historic person; but theirs is a hidden Jesus. Rudolph Bultmann, the foremost champion of Form Criticism, doubts altogether that the true personality of the historic Jesus can be discovered from the fragmentary Gospel stories. In the realm of dogmatic theology, Bultmann acknowledges his indebtedness to the early dialectical theology of Karl Barth. And yet this emphasis on the non-historical aspects of Christ presents a new and dangerous challenge to the classical Christian position that maintains that Jesus was wholly human and wholly divine. A retrospective look reveals that this issue has been the battle line for orthodox Christianity through the centuries, frequently necessitating the calling of a church council.

2. *The Importance of Christology*

Although the liberal movement remained essentially evangelical, there was a strong trend in historical liberalism, aided by scientific humanism, to reject the divinity of Christ; a trend to which some scholars yielded. It became the task of Karl Barth to restore the classical Christian position. He contended that the Christ assumed not only human nature, but also *fallen* human nature, which is the only human nature we know. Christ became in all points as we are.

Christology thus assumes a new importance. Here the lines of Christian theology converge, the incarnation becoming once more the central point of Christian thought, giving meaning and substance to all other concepts. For the Christian, God is not a hidden deity. He does not enwrap himself in veils of mystery awaiting man to discover him. But God is constantly seeking to reveal himself, to break through, to make himself known. The idea of *human quest* is not dominant in the Bible, which speaks of divine visitation and divine revelation. God takes the initiative. He is an active, dynamic force, always seeking ways to manifest himself to men. Incarnation is the climax of this self-revelation. For it is the divine destiny to enter into the human. The eternal Logos needs the human, the human language, and the human nature, to make himself known. Since the human nature is the only nature we know, God has to become man. The wise do not question whether Christ is divine, but rather, they ask, What is God like?

For Christianity the incarnation and the cruifixion are the moments in history when the true nature of God is revealed. It is not only in the nature of God to create and to reveal himself, but also to redeem his creation. The concept of redemption logically follows any idea of God in Christ.

II. THE DOCTRINE OF THE LOGOS AS A FUNDAMENTAL CONCEPT IN CHRISTOLOGY

The philosophical doctrine of the Logos plays a large part in Christological inquiry. In Greek philosophy it is conceived as the principle of reason ruling the world; in the Old Testament it is the wisdom, the glory, the spirit of God; in Philo it assumed a leading conception of thought and thus became more than a principle of reason: it became the divine dynamic, the energy of the self-revealing God. The Logos becomes central in interpreting the essential nature and character of Jesus, the Lord, in the New Testament.

1. *The Idea of the Logos in Greek Philosophy*

A history of the Logos-idea may begin with Heraclitus of Ephesus (c. 535-475 B.C.), who represents a mystical reaction against the materialism of the Ionian philosophers. For him the visible world is a symbolic system which half conceals and half reveals the reality. This truth or reality is the divine soul of the world, whose life is manifested in the endless cycle of birth and death, of becoming, change, decay, and renewal. There is *one* Logos, the same throughout the world, which is itself homogeneous and one. This wisdom we may win by searching within ourselves. The divine soul is "Nature," the cosmic process; it is God; it is the life-principle; it is the Logos, the divine Law, or the Will of God. This Logos is the immanent reason of the world; existing from all time. The Logos keeps the stars in their course. It is the hidden harmony which underlies the discords and antagonisms of existence. There is no trace in Heraclitus of a transcendent God, whose reason or will the Logos could be. The system is rather a form of pantheism, with a strong mystical element.

2. *The Idea of the Logos in Hebrew Thought*

Jewish thinkers were not concerned with the concept of the "Word of the Lord" until the tendency arose to personify the self-revealing activity of Jehovah. The earlier books of the Old Testament connect the operation of *Memra* with three ideas: creation, providence, and revelation. The tendency to personify the activities of Jehovah is seen in the expressions used about the Angel, the Name, the Glory, and, above all, the Wisdom of God. Similar language about the Word is found in the frequent phrase, "the word of the Lord came to me." The personification, however, is poetical rather than metaphysical.

In the later books, the conception of Wisdom tends to displace that of the Word, bringing the Jewish idea nearer the Greek. In Job, Wisdom is the hidden purpose which God is working out in man's existence—the grand secret of the life known only to God. In Proverbs, Wisdom is the cardinal virtue. Wisdom was the active agent in the creation of the world.

Philo blends Greek and Jewish ideas about the Logos. His Logos is a combination of the Platonic ideas and Stoic universal causality. He takes over the main Stoic conception, but detaches it from materialism, and tries to harmonize it with the Platonic theory that visible things are only instances of realities laid up in the intelligible world. His Logos is much like Plato's idea of the Good, except that it is regarded as creatively active. Jewish thought had been in danger of separating the Creator so completely from his creation as to produce an intolerable dualism. This tendency had been mitigated by poetical personification. Philo fixed these poetical symbols, and turned them from poetry to metaphysics. Philo's Logos is an intermediary between God and the world; he is the principle of revelation.

3. The Idea of the Logos in the New Testament

It is on this Philonic interpretation of the Logos that the writer of the Fourth Gospel builds. The Logos for the first time becomes a personal being, even before it becomes flesh in Jesus. The Logos is the means through which God is imparting to men his own divine energy. "In the beginning was the Word, and the Word was with God, and the Word was God" (John 1:1). The conception of Christ as a cosmic principle is dominant in the mind of Paul. To Paul, Christ was "the image of the invisible God; in him the *plērōma* of the Godhead dwells in bodily form; he was the agent of creation, and the immanent Spirit "through whom are all things;" he pre-existed in the form of God; all things are summed up in him, he is all in all. His reign is co-extensive with the world's history; he is the life-giving Spirit, abiding in the souls of his disciples, forming himself in them, and transforming them into his likeness, enlightening them and uniting them in one body with himself.

The author of the Fourth Gospel assumed that those to whom he wrote were acquainted with Philo's conception of the Logos. He maintained that from all eternity, before time began, the Logos *was.* He is supra-temporal, not simply the spirit of the world. The Logos is the light of men as life. From all eternity the Logos was divine; He assumed flesh at a particular point in history.

From this conception of the Logos all discussions are cast in a certain light. The questions that agitated the minds of Justin, Irenaeus, Tertullian, Clement, Origen, Paul of Samosata, and all the other great thinkers of the first four hundred years of the Christian church, were not the ones as to whether Christ was the Logos or whether there was a philosophically sound principle called the Logos—these things were assumed; the questions that agitated the minds of these great thinkers were whether this Logos was God Himself, a depotentiated and subordinate God, or a portion of God. The point of view that won the historic struggle maintained against formidable opposition that in Jesus was the very God himself.

4. *The Idea of the Logos among Contemporary Theologians*

Among contemporary theologians such as Barth, Brunner, and Tillich, the Logos is in no sense an abstract philosophical idea about God. It is God in communication. Paul Tillich says, " 'God manifest'—the mystery of the divine abyss expressing itself through the divine Logos—this is the meaning of the symbol, the 'Word of God.' " [1]

Brunner says, "Jesus is the Logos. He is the Word God has to speak to us." [2] Jesus the Logos, for Brunner, is an act of God's self-manifestation. Barth maintains that the terms "Son of God" and "Word of God" can be used interchangeably, emphasizing different phases of the same reality. This Word or Son is the eternal God in communication.

The Logos doctrine came into the New Testament as an apologetic move. Philo tried to fit the Old Testament into a current philosophical system. The writer of the Fourth Gospel seized upon it as an opportunity to relate the Christ to both the Old Testament Word of God and current Greek philosophy. It seems that contemporary theology has arrived at a point where it is not so much interested in the Logos doctrine of Greek philosophy as it is in the Old Testament doctrine of the Word. In some ways the Logos of Greek philosophy was actually an effort to avoid theism by positing something less than a God. This Logos was understood to be merely a principle of reason.

Today the doctrine of the Word of God is based on a simpler formulation. God, the transcendent, needs some means of communication; his Word is that means; that Word became personal and compelling in Jesus Christ. This is not Greek philosophy; this is Judeo-Christian tradition. In many ways the Scripture that says that "God was in Christ reconciling the world to himself" appears to be more satisfactory than that which says the "Logos became flesh and dwelt among us."

---

[1] From *Systematic Theology*, Vol. I, p. 159, by Paul Tillich; copyright 1951, The University of Chicago Press, Chicago.

[2] From *The Mediator*, p. 232, by Emil Brunner; copyright, 1947, by W. L. Jenkins, The Westminster Press. Used by permission.

III. THE TRINITY AS THE STRUCTURAL CONCEPT OF GOD'S THREEFOLD MANIFESTATION

The extensive literature of the Patristic period of the ancient Christian church bears witness to a consuming interest in Christology. In the Western Church this interest was not maintained in any continuous way, but it certainly was a lively issue in the Greek Church. Several Councils were forced to deal with the problem of Christology. If the Councils did not always reach a definite creed, heroic efforts were certainly made in that direction.

1. *The Trinity and Origen*

Christological speculation in this period was largely carried on within the framework of the Nicene Creed. One Council after another reaffirmed the Trinitarian formula of Nicaea. In the Eastern Church the first great thinker to come forth with definite Trinitarian ideas was Origen. In his masterful theological work, *De Principiis,* he defined the Trinity: "The Father is the principle of Existence, the Son of reason, and the Spirit of that which makes holy." [3] He followed Nicaea in asserting one Divine substance; the Son and the Holy Spirit were of the same substance of the Father. He formulated what later became known as the vertical Trinity. The Father was above all, the Son was below the Father and was subservient to the Father. For this and other reasons he was officially condemned at the Second Council of Constantinople in A.D. 553. As a heretic he had no standing in the Christian community and his influence in the East waned.

2. *Patristic Period*

The Christians of the Patristic period were forced to work within the limits of their own culture. Every educated Greek

---

[3] *De Principiis,* quoted in Harnack's *History of Dogma,* p. 155.

knew Aristotle. Aristotle had once defined God as pure Being. As pure Being, God was infinite. He was limited by infinity. He could not transcend his infinity and become finite. On the other hand man was a human being. He was limited by his finiteness. He could not become infinite. The Greek thinkers used practical wisdom to solve this difficulty. On logical terms God could not become man. But he did. The events happened. He did reveal himself in his Son. Hence the Greek thinkers combined a logical proposition with a fact of history and came up with the paradox, the phrase, "The God-Man." Christ was the God-Man.

Various thinkers such as Origen, Theodore of Mopsuestia, Cyril, Honorius, Dioscurus, and others, tried in vain to solve the question of the unity of the two persons in Christ, from the point of view of the soul, mind, body, and will. Each attempt was a matter of relative degree. In each case the question was, "How much in Christ was divine and how much was human?" The question was set by the culture patterns of Greek thought and life. Our thought on the same old problem will reflect the predominant thought pattern of our age and culture. While this endlessly discussed matter of Christology was going on in the ancient church, practical wisdom and piety reverted to the paradox of "The God-Man." And Christ came to us in history with the full assertion of his humanity and divinity. The Greeks rightly saw that Christology was vitally related to the incarnation and to the whole doctrine of Christian salvation. The Christian doctrine of the atonement depends upon the divine nature of Christ.

3. *Augustine*

Before A.D. 553 considerable dissatisfaction was expressed regarding Origen's concept of the Trinity. The solution of the problem was made in the Western Church. Long before the Second Council of Constantinople, Augustine had started to work on a new formulation of the Trinity. Unlike his many other writings, his great work on the Trinity was not called forth in the heat of controversy. It was a work of continuous growth from the years A.D. 400 to 416. From the latter date, Augustine's formulation of the Trinitarian doctrine was definitive in the Western Church and also in the Eastern Church. He begins,

> That the Father, and the Son, and the Holy Spirit intimate a divine unity of one and the same substance in an individual equality; and therefore they are not three Gods, but one God; although the Father hath begotten the Son, and so He who is the Father is not the Son; and the Son is begotten by the Father and so He who is Son is not the Father; and the Holy Spirit is neither Father nor Son, but the Holy Spirit of the Father and the Son, Himself also co-equal with the Father and the Son, and pertaining to the Unity of the Trinity.[4]

The position reached by Augustine later became known as the horizontal Trinity. There was only one substance of Godhead. The Father, Son, and Holy Spirit were all on the same level and co-equal. They moved as a unity. He maintained that one could not confound the persons or divide the substance.

Augustine made use of the Latin word *personae;* a word taken over from the Roman drama. *Personae* were the successive roles which an actor played in a drama. The actor was the same and his identity was concealed by a false face, yet the roles he played were various. In applying this to the Trinity, there was one divine substance, and the Father, Son, and Holy Spirit were different aspects of the divine substance.

While Augustine was concerned with the relationship of

---

[4] Augustine, *On the Trinity,* Book I, Chapter 4.

the three persons in the Trinity, he showed very little interest in the problems of Christology. To be sure, he was influenced by Paul, but he never caught any of the spirit of Paul's Christ-mysticism. All of Augustine's writings are pervaded with a God-mysticism. This is perfectly evident in the *Confessions*. If a mystic is one who has fallen in love with God, the object of Augustine's devotion and affection in the *Confessions* is God and God alone. He often says that he wants nothing more. He did give us a new workable definition of the Trinity. This influence has been felt in the Western Church. As in the East, the problems of Christology have been worked out within the framework of the Christian doctrine of the Trinity.

The fact of the Trinity was an unreasoned fact of experience. The disciples had personal relations with God the Father, Jesus the Son, and the Holy Spirit as Comforter. The experience drove them to a formulation of the Doctrine of the Trinity. Through philosophy and the thought life of the church it was expressed in a creed. Dr. Edward H. Pruden put it simply in a sermon when he said, "I am husband to my wife, father to my children, and pastor to my church, —three expressions of one personality,—but always one and the same person." [5]

IV. THE INCARNATION AND THE REVELATION OF GOD

We turn now to this most fundamental of issues in Christology. Just what was the relationship of God and man in Jesus? In what sense was he God and in what sense was he man?

The early centuries with all of their heresies, controversies, and Councils were concerned with these points and the pres-

---

[5] From *Interpreters Needed*, p. 72, by E. H. Pruden; copyright, 1951. The Judson Press, Philadelphia.

ent status of the problem cannot be understood without at least a passing knowledge of this background. It is much too general, but perhaps not completely unfair, to say that throughout all of these years the main stream of Christian theology was determined to hold on to Christ as both truly man and very God. The formulations of the various Councils and the proscribing of the many heresies are to be understood against the backdrop of this kind of motivation.

1. *Gnosticism and Docetism*

Two early trends in Christological thought, the Gnostic and Adoptianist were rejected. Gnosticism (and the related Docetism) denied the reality of Christ's physical nature. Gnostics said that redemption came by special knowledge, *gnōsis,* and Christ became the center of a mysterious cult of knowledge. They could not see spirit and matter in opposition, and so the docetic position that denied the reality of the flesh of Jesus was inevitable. Gnosticism was rejected for this very reason—in it Christ was not a man. The error of Adoptianism was on the other side of the issue. Adoptianists said that Jesus was a man, chosen, tested, then adopted and made divine. This was rejected because of the insistence that Christ *became* divine, and because of the denial of any pre-existence of the Son. The main stream of Christian theology held that this challenged the belief that Christ was truly God.

2. *Monarchianism*

Monarchianism was another early movement of thought that was later rejected; only to reappear in our time as a form of liberalism. Monarchists (either dynamic or modalistic) were insistent about the oneness of God and wanted to safeguard Christianity against any ditheistic tendencies. To them Christ became a more or less temporary divinity—neither pre-existently nor post-resurrectedly divine. But here again rejection was inevitable—orthodoxy did not want a temporary divinity.

3. Arianism

Perhaps Arianism is the best known of all the earlier heretical movements because its consequences were viewed with such seriousness. Arius began with a transcendent monotheism that posited God as perfect and infinite. Such a God could have no contact with the world. The Son was created as a kind of mediator of creation so that God would not have the despised contact. There was a time therefore when God was alone, and there was no actual identity between the Father and the Son. Arius insisted on the humanity of Jesus, but would not grant him a human soul. The Council of Nicaea in A.D. 325 condemned Arianism. The main stream of Christian theology did not want a kind of demi-God, or half-man and half-God. The Nicene Creed insisted that God and Jesus were of one substance (*homoousion*) and that Jesus was in an eternal, organic relation to the Godhead. Athanasius was the great champion of the Nicene formulation and said the Father and Son were "like in substance and like in all things." "The Son's place," said he, "is in the sphere of essential Godhead."

4. Apollinarianism

The Council of Constantinople in 381 affirmed the Nicene Creed against another heresy, Apollinarianism. Apollinaris accepted Jesus as one with God and then went on to give serious thought to the significance of his manhood. What he arrived at was a humanity that was something less than full. He felt that God-man was an impossibility, and so he denied that Christ's humanity was full or entire. His body and soul might have been human, but his spirit was replaced with the Logos. However, he went beyond even this and said that his flesh itself was deified and thus not consubstantial with ours. The Council rejected Apollinarian thought because it denied any real incarnation. It destroyed Christ's full humanity and saw the divine and human as two natures incapable of combination. The main stream was insisting on the full humanity of Jesus and thus the full reality of an incarnation.

5. *Nestorianism*

The Nestorian controversy next comes into view. The Nestorians said that God was present in Jesus, but in much the same way as he was in the prophets and other great men, not by nature but by grace. Nestorius resented the attempts to make Mary the mother of God and insisted that she bore an organ of the Godhead, not the Godhead itself. The net result of his thought was that the man Jesus was kept in sharp contrast with God the Word. Cyril of Alexandria opposed him, maintaining that God assumed flesh in Jesus and that he was "one out of two natures." "As soul and body are one in us, so Godhead and manhood were made one in Christ." The Council of Ephesus in A.D. 431 grew out of these difficulties. It is not considered to be the most productive of profound thought, but what it determined was this: that Christ represents a union of two natures. He is consubstantial with us and with God. The main stream had rejected any attempts to separate man as not worthy of God's indwelling.

6. *Eutychianism*

The Council of Chalcedon dealt with the Eutychian controversy that said that there were two natures before the incarnation but only one after it. The union in Christ produced just one nature. Chalcedon reaffirmed Nicaea and said that there were two natures in Christ, "two natures united without change, without confusion, without separation, without distinction." However, there was not the unity of a single personal life. Growing out of this position which opened the door for a type of dualism were the monophysite and monothelite difficulties. These movements were determined to affirm one nature and one will in Christ. The Council of Constantinople in A.D. 553 said that there were two natures in Christ, but that they were distinguishable only in theory. The Sixth Council in 680 declared that there were two wills in Christ, but that they were not in opposition, the human was obedient to the divine.

These early centuries set the framework into which later Christological discussions would fall. They represent a determination to affirm the full humanity of Jesus and at the same time to affirm with equal certainty his full divinity. At the close of this period it still remained for someone to work out the sound basis for the unity of a single personal life in Jesus, but it had been determined that this unity could not be at the expense of one of the natures.

7. *The Present Day*

This is not primarily a historical essay, so with this early background covered we shall skip over many important years and come to our present day and the options that are now offered.

Barth and Brunner have made tremendous contributions in this area of thought. Barth maintains that the Trinity is rooted in the nature of revelation itself. "God reveals Himself. He reveals Himself through Himself. He reveals Himself." [6] God reveals Himself as Lord.

> He comes as the angel to Abraham. He speaks through Moses and prophets. He is in Christ. Revelation in the Bible does not mean a minus, a something over against God. It means the equal of God, a repetition of God. Revelation

---

[6] From *The Doctrine of the Word of God,* p. 340, by Karl Barth; T. and T. Clark, Edinburgh, 1936.

is, of course, the predicate of God, but in such a way that this predicate coincides exactly with God Himself. He himself is not only Himself but also what He creates and achieves in men.[7]

The meaning of the doctrine of the Trinity is not that there are three personalities in God, but that there are three modes of being; threeness in oneness. God the Father as Creator; God the Son as Reconciler; God the Holy Spirit as Redeemer.

Brunner operates on very much the same basis as Barth. He says that the Father is the origin and content of the revelation, the Son is the mediator of the revelation, and the Holy Spirit is the present reality of that revelation.[8] "We have the Father through the Son, in the Son; but we do not have the Father alongside of the Son, and the Son alongside of the Father. We have the Son through the Spirit in the Spirit; but we ought not to have the Spirit alongside the Son, and the Son alongside of the Spirit." [9] Thus he emphasizes the threeness and the oneness. D. M. Baillie has suggested that these options fall into three general categories: Anhypostasia, Kenosis, and Leadership and Lordship. We shall look at them one by one.

a. *Anhypostasia.* Under Anhypostasia are included those Christological systems which deny the full human personality of Jesus. His was a divine personality living in impersonal humanity. A divine spirit is affixed to a human body. This was the position of Nestorius, who said Mary mothered only the flesh, not the divine personality. It would appear that all movements in this direction are the result of hesitancy to deal with the paradox of wholly human and wholly divine at the same time. Anhypostasia gets around this para-

---

[7] *Ibid.,* p. 343.
[8] From *The Christian Doctrine of God*, pp. 206-207, by Emil Brunner; published by The Westminster Press. Used by permission.
[9] *Ibid.,* p. 217.

dox by saying in effect that Jesus was not wholly human at all. He was divine personality in impersonal human flesh. Baillie's criticism is apt when he says of these thinkers that they are unable to conceive of a human personality completely dependent on God,—such a personality would be divine, not human. Baillie reminds them that though such dependence is not a denial of personality (actually it is personality at its best) it is rather a denial of independence.

b. *Kenosis.* Under Kenosis are those systems which speak of the divine as emptying itself of that which makes it divine in order to take on human form. In Jesus, God has laid aside his divine attributes in favor of human ones. Put bluntly, in Jesus, God ceases to be divine. Kenosis presents its problems. It seems to say that the divine was completely emptied into the human and so literally there was no God in the heavens during the life of Jesus. It seems also to say that this emptying of the divine was at best temporary, and on the death of Jesus there is no longer any Christ in existence, just God. These two difficulties alone place the systems under serious question.

c. *Leadership and Lordship.* Under Leadership and Lordship falls principally the Christology of Heim. He sees Christ as a Leader given to us by God, a Leader to lead us to God. He leads us through direct personal contact and this contact is still possible today. The essential element thus becomes the personal relationship between the follower and the Leader. Although interesting, this Christological position has very little merit for us as it lacks any real discussion or comprehension of the nature of Christ and God.

It becomes apparent that the real issue in all of this is just what essential manhood is and in what sense Jesus had it. According to Hodgson, the human self or soul suggests the conscious subject of experience. These experiences are, of course, received through the instrumentality of the body.

It was this that the divine Logos consented to be, a conscious subject of experiences received through a human body. However, there is no indication in Hodgson's thought that this was anything other than a divine Mind being a subject of experience mediated through a human body.

Karl Barth makes no such distinction between the body and the divine Mind. On the contrary he insists that Christ was human in every detail, that his was not simply human nature, but fallen human nature. He is not particularly interested in the historical details of Jesus' life because they were just common things. His human life, after all, was not the revelation of God but the concealment of God. So Barth accepts the fullness of humanity in Jesus, but cannot posit it as that through which God is revealed. God remained behind the scenes in Jesus until the resurrection and the post-resurrection period.

Brunner draws a fine line of distinction between what he calls human personality and the Divine Person. The human personality was accessible to everyone, but behind lies a Divine Person. The human personality is the veiling, the incognito of God. It is difficult to see how Brunner could escape the charge of anhypostasis leanings. The Divine Person is certainly something in place of a human person. He cannot see a human person or personality as a revelation; it merely veils that which is behind it.

Barth would agree with Brunner's affirmation that only through God is knowledge of God possible. Revelation alone is the source of such knowledge. They both would go on to say that Jesus was God giving himself and revealing himself, but they both feel compelled to add that this revelation was through something other than his humanness, for this is just the veiling, the incognito of God. They both seem relatively unaware of the fact that it was the human, historical life of Jesus, that led the early Christians to think of him as God, or as his revelation. It almost seems for these dialectical theologians that if Jesus is to be divine or the revelation of the divine, the human must be negated. It is to be remembered that Barth and Brunner are motivated in this by their idea of a transcendent God, as opposed to an easy familiarity with him.

Up to this point, then, we have found no system of thought that does complete justice to the humanity and divinity of Christ at one and the same time in the unity of a single personal life. That is the contribution which D. M. Baillie makes through his intriguing application of the paradoxical doctrine of grace. He roots his thought back to what he calls the Christian understanding of the paradoxical nature of God which enables us to say, "Not I, but the grace of God." It is the divine nature of God by which he gives himself to dwell in man that enables man, by his own free will to choose God's will, yet to acknowledge that this very choice is of God. This activity of God, his grace, is not the negation of humanness or human will; it is its fulfillment. When you bring this understanding of the paradoxical nature of God and of his grace to bear upon the paradox of the incarnation it sheds great light.

Gospel references can be multiplied almost without end where Jesus says something very similar to "Not I, but God." His actions God accepted as based on human choice, yet their source was always God. In Galatians 2:20 (KJV), Paul says, "I live; yet not I, but Christ liveth in me." What this means to the Christian is perhaps what the incarnation means to Christ. Let it be remembered that this application of the paradox of grace is not to be misconstrued as a substitute for the incarnation. Typical questions such as: "Was Christ divine because he lived a perfect life? or did he live a perfect life because he was divine?" do no harm here. The incarnation or prevenience of God is assumed. Baillie is not trying to substitute a new formula for that of Chalcedon, but he is trying to understand it, to understand how two natures can work together in the unity of a single personal life. He contends that the problem fades as the existence of a paradox in the doctrine of the incarnation is openly acknowledged. Thus, some degree of understanding can be attained when the significance of the "paradox of grace" is realized.

This position has many distinct advantages. One does not have to speak of a veiling of God or incognito of God. It is assumed that Jesus is God. Nor does one have to posit a kind of mutilated humanity. It is assumed that Jesus is a man in every sense that we say that we are men. The paradox involved in those statements is not explained away, but understood. This position also has the advantage of salvaging all of Jesus' life and teachings as a revelation of God. It is not just what he was as the Logos of God and not just his resurrection and post-resurrection life that reveals God. It is all of him,—his life, his teachings, his death, and his resurrection. Finally, this position has the advantage of eliminating some of the distinctions between the Jesus of history and the Christ of faith. They are one and the same—that is the essential truth of the incarnation. "God was in Christ reconciling the world unto himself."

This is what Christ as Incarnate Word means to us: God communicating with us and giving himself to us through and by the whole of Jesus' life.

Summary

A brief sketch like this, of a tremendous subject, must leave one with the feeling that more has been left unsaid than has been said. We have been thinking about Jesus Christ as Incarnate Word and Eternal Son. We have concluded that Jesus was the Incarnate Word, not in the sense of a logos of Greek philosophy in which Jesus became a visible manifestation of an abstract principle of reason, but in the sense of Jesus becoming God's Word of communication to us through our own kind—manhood at its finest and best. We have concluded that Jesus is the Eternal, Pre-existent Son in the sense that it was part of the very nature of God from all time to communicate and give himself to us, and so the divine in Jesus was pre-existent just as there has always been a God. We also affirm that on Jesus' death and resurrection his individuality did not cease, but that he continues as the Eternal Son.

BIBLIOGRAPHY

Baillie, Donald M., *God Was in Christ*. New York: Charles Scribner's Sons, 1955. 230 pp.

Barth, Karl, *The Doctrine of the Word of God*. Edinburgh: T. & T. Clark, 1936. 2 vols.

Brunner, Emil, *The Mediator*. The Macmillan Company, 1934. 621 pp.

Lowry, Charles W., *The Trinity and Christian Devotion*. New York: Harper & Brothers, 1946. 162 pp.

McGiffert, Arthur Cushman, *A History of Christian Thought*. New York: Charles Scribner's Sons, 1932–33. 2 vols.

Niebuhr, Reinhold, *The Nature and Destiny of Man*. New York: Charles Scribner's Sons, 1945. 2 vols.

Orr, James, *The Progress of Dogma*. A. C. Armstrong and Son, 1902. 365 pp.

Scott, E. F., *The Fourth Gospel*. Edinburgh: T. & T. Clark, 1906. 379 pp.

Tillich, Paul, *Systematic Theology*. Chicago: The University of Chicago Press, 1951. 2 vols.

Wolfson, Harry A., *The Philosophy of the Church Fathers*. Cambridge: Harvard University Press, 1956.

IV

A CHRISTIAN DOCTRINE OF MAN: MAN'S ESSENTIAL NATURE

—◆—•◼•◼•—◆—

W. ALVIN PITCHER

RECENT EVENTS indicate that man continues to destroy him-self in spite of his increasing knowledge and wealth. When we consider "what man has made of man" we are shocked. Men deliberately have put to death millions of those who share their humanity. Millions literally destroy them-selves by wishing to be what they cannot be. Mental sickness, alcoholism, dope addiction, and juvenile delinquency point to this self-destruction.

Men are enslaved by the feeling that they must do what other people do. Few seem able to set their own standards. What they do, say, wear, and see is determined largely by what others do, say, wear, and see. What men think they should be is prescribed by friends, demands of the office, and the heroes and heroines of television, radio, movie, and comic book. Even those who wish to do things in a different way are unable to resist the pressure to conform.

At the same time, many feel that the pattern of life set by

these "models" is not necessary for the health of our civilization. At least they are not sure that such values and activities are required to keep our standard of living high. They even wonder if the high standard of living is worth the human cost. They ask, "Are we achieving higher wages and more services by organizing life in such a way that man is prevented from being what he is intended to be?"

There is growing evidence, also, that a spiritual vacuum has been created by "what man has made of man." Without deep religious loyalties, men either strive blindly to find a new cause to serve or cling doggedly to old ideas and habits. Communism represents the fanatical search for the new. Fascism is the fanatical effort to keep the old.

Finally, the ultimate challenge to the Christian view of man is made by those who claim that man is not intended to be anything. He creates, they say, his own goals. What man is meant to be is whatever he is able to make of himself. He creates his own essence.

Now there is some truth to the belief that man is meant to be what he can be. As we look back at history we see that man cannot do some things and remain man. But dare we wait to see whether or not man will destroy himself? Dare we wait for history to test which view of man is better? Dare we wait to see what man is intended to be? We do not think we can afford to take this chance. Fully aware that they are God's judgments and not ours, we would prefer to try to anticipate the judgments of history. We would prefer to try to discover as best we can what man is meant to be. We cherish the faith that man can know something about his essential nature. With this knowledge man may be better able to deal with his denial of this goal and with his false and true efforts to transform and to renew human existence. Without some knowledge of what he is intended to be, man has no place to begin. He has no way to judge between the better and worse. He has no way to evaluate the pressures upon him. He has no way to choose among the alternative patterns of life. He has no basis for creating new goals.

But knowledge of what man is intended to be, as discussed in this paper, is only the beginning. A more complete analysis would involve five stages. While we may talk about each stage separately, they represent five ways of looking at ourselves. No one stage is complete without the others.

1. Man as he is created to be—his essential nature or his goal.

2. Man's denial of his essential nature—man as a sinner. What are the created limitations of man? What are the aspects of his life for which he is responsible?

3. Man's life as an evidence of the struggle involving his goal, his denial of this goal (sin), and the contingencies of existence. What is happening to man? What can we expect of man in the present situation?

4. Man's life in faith—redeemed man. What is involved in man's redemption? What can and cannot be accomplished by Christian education and by the Christian faith? What is the role of education, and of the other agencies of character development in the realization of man's moral and spiritual nature?

5. Man's life in and beyond history—eschatological man. What is man's ultimate destiny and hope? How does man participate in the Kingdom of God?

While none of these stages is complete in itself, there is value in considering the first one, the essential nature of man, in this paper. In the past, Christians have referred to "what man is meant to be" or man's essential nature by the phrase "image of God." Therefore, in this paper we shall use the idea of the *Image of God* or "what man is intended to become" as the basis for our exploration of the Old Testament, the New Testament, Christian thinkers of the past and present, and non-Christian thinkers who are writing about the same problem. Finally we shall attempt our own formulation.

But first let us consider briefly the problems involved in setting forth a doctrine of man's goal or of his essential nature. There is no way to escape asking this question: Where do we look to find what man is meant to be? Do we look to man himself as we know him in our common sense experience or in the sciences? Or do we find what man is meant to be only in God's revealing acts, particularly in Christ. Is it in a study of Christ's deeds and teaching or in a personal union with Christ that our essential nature becomes evident?

In the second place, men have asked about the nature of the *Image of God*. Is it a power, something man possesses as he possesses the potentiality for speech? Is it a relation involving other men and God, so that like a friendship or marriage it involves more than one individual? Or does the *Image of God* exist as an intention or purpose in God? Is the image like the image in a mirror? Is its source outside us? Is it dependent upon a power within us to reflect the source?

Very closely related to this consideration is that of the content of the image. Does that which is designated by the *Image of God* or the created intention of man consist of man's rationality, freedom, rule over things, responsible action, or love?

In the fourth place, we ask about the structure of man's life in terms of body, mind, soul, and spirit. How is the image related to these aspects of man?

Finally, we shall ask about the significance of man's essential nature. Does it designate an original righteousness before man falls or a final attainment possible only in the mystery of a final consummation beyond history? Is it possible to use the knowledge of man's essential nature or ultimate goal as a guide to what can be expected of man in his sinful condition or in his life of faith?

I. THE IMAGE OF GOD IN MAN IN
THE OLD TESTAMENT

The following verses are contained in the scriptural accounts of creation:

> Then God said, "Let us make man in our image, after our likeness; and let them have dominion over the fish of the sea, and over the birds of the air, and over the cattle, and over all the earth, and over every creeping thing that creeps upon the earth." So God created man in his own image, in the image of God he created him; male and female he created them (Gen. 1:26-27).

> Then the Lord God formed man of dust from the ground, and breathed into his nostrils the breath of life; and man became a living being (Gen. 2:7).

In Genesis 5:1-2 we read also:

> This is the book of the generations of Adam. When God created man, he made him in the likeness of God. Male and female he created them. . . .

Let us assume that the words "image" and "likeness" mean an image "which is like;" i.e., that we have Hebrew parallelism here. The simple declaration of the Scriptures is that man in his creation was like God. He was created with something that made him like God and it was good (cf. Gen. 1:31). This is a tremendous affirmation in itself. It implies that man has a goal, that he is meant to be something, yet what the content of the *Image of God* is, is not at once clear.

There are three aspects of the Genesis story from which we can work directly to discover the content of the image: (1) the image or likeness; (2) the dominion over nature, and (3) the distinction between male and female.

The image may be said to consist of man's dominion over the creatures, a dominion arising from the powers with which he was and is invested and from the express appointment of God. God constituted man to rule over the earth. The Psalmist supports this view: "Thou hast given him [man] dominion over the works of thy hands; thou hast put all things under his feet . . ." (Ps. 8:6). However, while this does support the idea of the dignity of man's original state, it is not to be identified with the image, for the term "image" has a more specific meaning.

In Genesis 1:27 and 5:1-2 these statements occur: "Male and female he created them," and "When God created man, he made him in the likeness of God. Male and female he created them, and he blessed them and named them Man when they were created." Again this seems to be subordinate to the image or likeness; certainly it is not the whole content of the image. Nevertheless these statements do suggest that the image in some way designates a structure that includes within it what is required by the fact that we have man as male and female. Much has been made of this (as we shall see in discussing Karl Barth) to indicate that the image designates a relationship among persons. Thus, for the Old Testament the essential nature of man points to a relationship rather than something possessed by an individual in isolation.

Walter Eichrodt, in his *Theologie des Alten Testaments,* says

> If we remember the whole manner and fashion in which the Godhead is pictured in Genesis 1, how He appears from the first lines as a conscious and powerful will, and continually bears witness to Himself through insistent purposive creation, we shall be forced to find man's likeness to God as indicated by the author, in his spiritual superiority, which expresses itself not only in his higher rational endowment, but above all in his capacity for self-consciousness and self-determination. . . . The gift to man of the *imago dei* . . . implies nothing less than a connection with God through

which man, even as a sinner, remains a rational being capable of spiritual fellowship with God. His pre-eminence over all other creatures consists in the fact that as a conscious self he can be reached by God's work and thereby called to responsibility.[1]

Higher rational endowment, self-consciousness, and responsible self-determination may designate the powers of man referred to by the *Image of God*, but if so, we must look for the justification beyond Genesis in the Old Testament. It is no simple matter, however, to find a way to express what man is meant to be according to the Old Testament. For a long time scholars either found no unity in the Old Testament or were content to trace the development of religious ideas from the early primitive conceptions to the later mature understandings. More recently the emphasis has been upon unity. At the risk of oversimplification we, too, must attempt to find a way to state the central message of the Old Testament regarding man without claiming that this is the only view expressed. We shall attempt to find in the covenant relationship the content of the *Image of God*.

Having been created as "little less than God" (Ps. 8:5) with dominion over the earth and over all living things, man finds his fulfillment in obedience to the will of God. Frequently this life of obedience has been referred to as responsible existence. In the Old Testament the conditions laid down by God in his covenant require man's obedience to the law. "You shall walk in all the way which the LORD your God has commanded you, that you may live, and that it may go well with you . . ." (Deut. 5:33). But the law is not to be considered as something that can be completely grasped and formulated. Finally, we must say, "Let the words of my mouth and the meditation of my heart be acceptable in thy

---

[1] From *The Image of God in Man*, pp. 21-22, by David Cairns; copyright, 1953, by The Philosophical Library, New York.

sight, O LORD, my rock and my redeemer" (Ps. 19:14). We must say with Job, "I have uttered what I did not understand, things too wonderful for me, which I did not know. 'Hear, and I will speak; I will question you, and you declare to me.' I had heard of thee by the hearing of the ear, but now my eye sees thee . . ." (Job 42:3-5). The law of God in pointing to the righteousness of man is a response to the "righteousness of God" (the shape and the content of the activity of God). This response depends upon man's capacity to know and to do the will of God. This knowledge is given in the law and prophets (cf. Ex. 24:3-8; Jer. 11:1-10; 31:31-40). The response also involves man's will which, in the freedom granted by God's righteousness and established by the covenant relationship, is able to keep the covenant. Man's keeping of the covenant takes the form of trust in God (cf. Isa. 7:9; Gen. 15:6) and love of neighbor (cf. Lev. 19:17-18, 34).

Thus, although the command of God must always be conceived in a dynamic way, the law embodied in the decalogue points to the conditions under which the covenant is maintained and man is what he is created to be.

In this view of the message of the Old Testament, the *Image of God* in man consists of a continuing relationship of response to the continuing activity of God. The formal structure of the relationship is given by the notion of law. Guidance is given by the Ten Commandments and other expressions of the law. The concrete content is given by God in each concrete situation. Thus, the image or the essential nature of man cannot be conceived of apart from the present activity of God.

Furthermore, it is not possible to think of the image primarily as the possession of an individual. The covenant is maintained with a people of God represented by Israel or a saving remnant of Israel.

II. THE IMAGE OF GOD IN MAN IN
THE NEW TESTAMENT

As we move into the New Testament, as indeed we must, since this has always been considered the foundation of a Christian doctrine of man, we find two places to look for man's essential nature, and an intimation of a third. The intimation is in Paul's suggestion in Romans 1 that men whose knowledge of God is perverted are given up by God. It is implied that those who have a true knowledge of God, worshiping the Creator rather than the creature, would conform to God's decree without any thought of rebellion. They would do his will.

But our interest in the New Testament centers in the knowledge of Jesus, *the man,* and in the *new* man created by the response of faith in Jesus Christ. The words of Pilate, "Behold the man," point to the fact that Jesus is *the* man, the embodiment of what man is meant to be. Other statements point to Jesus Christ as providing knowledge of the *Image of God* in man. Paul indicates that "those whom he [God] foreknew he also predestined to be conformed to the image of his Son . . ." (Rom. 8:29) "who is the likeness of God" (2 Cor. 4:4). Thus, the Epistles are written to men who are "made in the likeness of God" (Jas. 3:9), who "are being changed into his likeness" (2 Cor. 3:18), or who are either admonished to "put on the new nature, created after the likeness of God in true righteousness and holiness" (Eph. 4:24), or informed that they "have put on the new nature, which is being renewed in knowledge after the image of its creator" (Col. 3:10).

Hence what man is meant to be is pointed to (1) by what Jesus Christ was, and (2) by the new man brought about by union with Christ.

We have the content of the essential nature of man portrayed, then, in Jesus Christ as a person—both in his deeds and words. Faith is rooted in confidence in God's mercy. Faith active in love of God and of all neighbors gives the general content of man's essential life. But we must not forget to ask this question: "Since Jesus was more than man, what in him represents something that we should not expect of ourselves?"

In Paul's Epistles the life of the new creature is described in connection with the image. The following are suggestive of what is to be put to death: immorality, impurity, passion, evil desire, covetousness, anger, wrath, malice, slander, foul talk from the mouth, lying, division (into Greek and Jew, circumcised and uncircumcised, barbarian, Scythian, slave and freeman), harshness of husbands with wives, and provocation of children by fathers (cf. Col. 3). This, of course, is only the negative aspect.

The following are to be put on: Compassion, kindness, lowliness, meekness, patience, forbearing one another, forgiving each other, love which binds everything together in perfect harmony, peace of Christ in your hearts, thanksgiving, the word of Christ as you teach and admonish one another, and as you sing psalms and hymns and spiritual songs with thankfulness in your hearts to God, the things that are above, gracious speech seasoned with salt, prayer, just and fair treatment of slaves, hearty work at your task, obedience of children to parents, the doing of everything in the name of the Lord, subjection of wives to husbands as is fitting in the Lord, love of husbands for wives, obedience of slaves to masters, and steadfastness in prayer, being watchful in it with thanksgiving. (cf. Col. 3).

In these descriptions of what man is to put off and to put on, we find the content of the *Image of God;* i.e., what man was created to be.

III. THE IMAGE OF GOD IN MAN IN
HISTORICAL THEOLOGY

Now let us examine the historical documents portraying the developing life of the church. There we find that the Christian doctrine of the "essential nature of man," or of the *Image of God,* or of "that which man is created to be" has had a long history. Many Christians have attempted to interpret the meaning of the relevant biblical statements. The life of the church has reflected these various understandings of the doctrine.

In the early church, the *Image of God* in man was almost exclusively defined as that which was distinctive of man. An effort was made to find what separated man from other species of animals. Thus, the peculiarly human powers of man were chosen from among the following: reason, freedom, speech, and rule over all other creatures. This does not mean that the notion that man's essential nature is related to the self-imparting love of God is absent in the first century and a half. However, with Irenaeus, the distinction on which the medieval doctrines of man rest was established once and for all as a problem.

Irenaeus distinguished between the *Image of God* and the *likeness of God.* The *Image of God* designated man's rationality and freedom. The *likeness of God* is established by faith. Where there is faith, there is repentance and obedience to the demands of the Decalogue and of the Two Commandments. The distinction between "image" and "likeness" is important, because it provides one basis for discussing the *Image of God* after the fall. What is lost through sin? Is sinful man without the "image?" Or is sinful man without a quality of the "image" that can be designated as the "likeness?" Sometimes one may feel that writers make such distinctions in order to differ with one another. Usually, however, they are trying to point out a real problem. The real question here is this: "What can sinful man do by himself? Has he lost all of his capacity to know and to do the good? That is to say, has he lost both the 'image' and the 'likeness'? Or, does he retain some capacity ('image') but not all ('likeness')?" These questions cannot be avoided. They continue to be raised in the thought of the church. Hence, as we turn now to consider Thomas Aquinas, perhaps more of the meaning of Irenaeus' discussion will be discovered.

Thomas Aquinas asks about the capacity of man to know what he is meant to be on the basis of rational perception; i.e., the ordinary knowledge he has about himself. In Thomas, man has the power, called synteresis, to judge between good and bad. To be sure his judgment about what is good and what is bad in a given situation is not always adequate unless it has been properly trained or habituated. But man's reason is able to know his proper end.

In the Augustinian tradition, including Luther and Calvin, however, what man is meant to be is known only in Christ. Calvin contends this knowledge is secured in two ways: first, by our knowledge of what Jesus Christ was, and second, by virtue of the action of God in Christ in us, such that our reason is able to understand our true nature. Thus, in Calvin there is no true knowledge of man without knowledge of God and no true knowledge of God until man recognizes his true condition. The knowledge of God is a knowledge of God in his creation and in his redemption (i.e., in Jesus Christ). But the knowledge of God in creation, and thus of man's created nature, is only possible through the knowledge of God in Jesus Christ.

Thus, the *Image of God* is found in Christ or by man only when in a certain relationship to God through Christ. The nature of the image is described either by a purpose or an intention in God or by an active relation between God and man. The image is not a power or a possession of man. The significance of this difference is seen in the Protestant critique of Irenaeus and Aquinas. If the image is a power, it is implied that this power in man can be the basis not only for knowledge of his own nature but also for movement toward its fulfillment. For Aquinas:

> Since man is said to be made in the image of God by reason of his intellectual nature, he is the most perfectly like God according as his intellectual nature can most imitate God. Now the intellectual nature imitates God chiefly in this, that God understands and loves Himself. Therefore the image of God may be considered in man in three ways. First, inasmuch as man possesses a natural aptitude for understanding and loving God; and this aptitude consists in the very nature of the mind, which is common to all men. Secondly, inasmuch as man actually or habitually knows and loves God, though imperfectly; and this image consists in the conformity of grace. Thirdly, inasmuch as man knows God actually and loves him perfectly; and this image consists in the likeness of glory.[2]

In his commentary on Genesis, Luther criticizes the divines who have defined the image in terms of the intellect illuminated by faith, memory confirmed by hope and constancy, and will adorned by love. He criticizes the former interpretations because they do not fully take into account the corruption of these natural endowments. In Adam, these endowments were present in a quite different way.

> All his senses, both internal and external, were the most perfect and the most pure. His intellect was most clear, his memory most complete, and his will the most sincere, and accompanied with the most charming society, without any fear of death and without any care or anxiety whatsoever. To

---

[2] From *The Basic Writings of St. Thomas Aquinas*, I.93.4, Anton C. Pegis, ed.; copyright, 1945, by Random House, New York.

these internal perfections of Adam was added a power of body, and of all his limbs, so beautiful and so excellent that therein he surpassed all other animate natural creatures.[3]

Whereas man now is corrupt, for Luther, Adam possessed the image of God in its moral substance or nature. He "not only knew God and believed Him to be good, but . . . he lived also a life truly divine. . . ."[4]

This life divine, a life lived in terms of the *Image of God,* is restored to us through the gospel. In its perfection, not in this life, but in the Kingdom of the Father, "will our will be truly free and good, our memory constant and perfect. Then will it come to pass, also, that all creatures shall be more subject unto us than ever they were unto Adam in paradise."[5]

For Calvin, the image designates something actually present in man as well as the divinely planned end of creation. The latter exists in God's intention in spite of anything man does. But Calvin also says that man is in God's image when he reflects back in gratitude God's glory. Thus he has all three elements in the image: (1) a power of structure of being, (2) a relation of response to God's activity, and (3) an intention or purpose in the mind of God.

In Calvin's discussions in the *Institutes,* soul and body are the two distinguishable elements of man. The proper seat of the *Image of God* is the soul, an immortal yet created essence. Spirit refers to that part of the soul that has been renewed to bear the *Image of God.* Nevertheless the glory of God is displayed in the external form of man that distinguishes him from the brutes and exalts him more nearly to God. Image and likeness both denote

---

[3] From *A Compend of Luther's Theology,* p. 81, edited by Hugh Thomson Kerr, Jr.; copyright, 1943, The Westminster Press. Used by permission.

[4] *Ibid.,* p. 82.

[5] *Ibid.,* p. 93.

the integrity which Adam possessed, when he was endued with a right understanding, when he had affections regulated by reason, all his senses governed in proper order, and when in the excellency of his nature, he truly resembled the excellence of his Creator.[6]

Calvin goes on, then, to point out that the way we best know the image is through the restoration of man's corrupted nature through Christ. The renewal of the *Image of God* is described by reference to Christ who "is all, and in all" (cf. Col. 3:10-11). "We see, now, how Christ is the most perfect image of God, to which being conformed, we are so restored that we bear the Divine image in true piety, righteousness, purity, and understanding." [7]

The soul has two faculties, the understanding and the will. The understanding discerns the good from the evil, and the just from the unjust. This faculty of understanding discovers by the light of reason what ought to be done and what ought not to be done. To the understanding, which is the principal or governing part, is added the faculty of the will, on which depends the significant act of choice.

The primitive condition of man was enobled with those eminent faculties; he possessed reason, understanding, prudence, and judgment, not only for the government of his life on earth, but to enable him to ascend even to God and eternal felicity. To these was added choice, to direct the appetites, and regulate all the organic motions; so that the will should be entirely conformed to the government of reason. In this integrity man was endued with free will, by which, if he had chosen, he might have obtained eternal life.[8]

The image, for Calvin, is not the possession of man. Rather,

---

[6] From *Institutes of the Christian Religion*, I.15.3, by John Calvin, translated by John Allen; copyright, 1935, Presbyterian Board of Education, Philadelphia.

[7] *Ibid.*, I.15.4.

[8] *Ibid.*, I.15.8.

it is as a reflection of God that man bears the image. The mirror that reflects God is the Word or Christ. God looks upon himself, so to speak, and beholds himself in man as in a mirror.[9] In God's constant renewing or support of man there is a special renewing that goes beyond the renewal of ordinary existence. This is a renewing of man after the image of God in Christ. Objectively it is grounded in the divine intention to which man with God's help may respond in thankful obedience. The pattern of obedience is rectitude or constant dependence upon the mercy of God. Obedience also involves the dominion of man over the world of animals and nature. In addition, the pattern of mutuality present in the relationship of Adam and Eve represents the intention of God for man. Immortality, the goal of man's earthly life, requires knowledge of God. This knowledge is twofold: knowledge of his mercy and knowledge of his will. Knowledge of his mercy, if it be steady and certain, is faith. Knowledge of his will, (the law), if it be real, is sanctification or righteousness.

In the *Commentary on Genesis,* Calvin sums up his view of man's creation and destiny:

> After the world had been created, man was placed in it as in a theatre, that he, beholding above him and beneath the wonderful works of God, might reverently adore their Author. Secondly, that all things were ordained for the use of man, that he, being under deeper obligation, might devote and dedicate himself entirely to obedience towards God. Thirdly, that he was endued with understanding and reason, that being distinguished from brute animals he might meditate on a better life and might even tend directly towards God whose image he bore engraven on his person.[10]

---

[9] *Calvin's Doctrine of Man,* "Sermon on Job," 10.7 f., p. 39, by T. F. Torrance; Lutterworth, London, 1949.

[10] From *Commentary on Genesis,* pp. 64-65, by John Calvin, translated by John King. Calvin Translation Society, Edinburgh, 1847.

IV. THE ESSENTIAL NATURE OF MAN OR THE IMAGE OF GOD IN MAN IN MODERN THOUGHT

With the development of modern science and philosophy, frequently the *Image of God* in man has been identified with the higher or rational part of man or with human nature at its best or in its universal characteristics. Increasingly the psychology of personality tries to describe a "mature" person. Carl Rogers who has developed the client-centered methods of psychotherapy finds himself unable to avoid asking the question: What is the goal of therapy? When is it successful? Mr. Rodgers has tried to describe the goal in terms of the needs and potentialities of man's nature. His concept of the "fully functioning person" [11] is roughly equivalent to the idea of the *Image of God*.

For Rodgers, a fully functioning person is one who (1) is open to experience, (2) expects the future to provide unforseen possibilities, and (3) has confidence in his capacity to handle whatever turns up without great stress and strain. In being open to experience, the fully functioning person is able to accept himself and what experience tells him about his potentialities and limitations. He does not need to be defensive, to reject, or to distort experience. When he is tired, he can admit that he is tired. When he feels tired, he *is* tired, and not merely feeling tired in order to escape something. When he is tired, he does not need to reject the feeling in order to appear to himself as strong and able.

Each moment is new for this person. He does not try to force his experience into preconceived patterns. He expects changes to occur in himself and in his experience. This

---

[11] This description of the fully functioning person is found in an unpublished paper by Carl Rogers, "The Concept of the Fully Functioning Person."

provides for adaptability rather than rigidity in meeting the recurring organismic needs (survival, enhancement, food, affection, sex, etc.).

This individual is also able to accept his "feeling" of what is right to do. This does not mean that the fully functioning person expects his organism to be infallible. However, since he is open to experience, all of the relevant data is sought and used. Errors and failures are quickly analyzed and corrected.

We are never quite sure, of course, whether this description by Mr. Rodgers represents the kind of person that is produced by his particular counseling procedures, or whether the counseling procedures are used because they help a person to become what, for one one reason or another, Mr. Rodgers wishes him to be. In either case, we wonder why we should accept this model for our lives.

In *The Courage to Be,* Paul Tillich helps us see more clearly the reason for our attempt to describe the essential nature of man. He can be taken to represent those who seek to use the Bible and the discoveries of modern science to describe human nature. In his description of anxiety, Tillich distinguishes two kinds: (1) essential anxiety and (2) sinful anxiety. Anxiety designates the painful feeling of not being able to preserve one's own being. This may take different forms, according as the special situation related to this feeling is one's existence, meaning, or morality. Corresponding to the threats to these three phases of one's self-affirmation are the anxious states designated by the threatening aspects of man's experiences: fate or death, meaninglessness or emptiness, and guilt or condemnation.

In the anxiety of fate and death, man feels driven through time, without a moment which does not vanish immediately. He feels homeless without any space that is really his own. He is subject to attacks by disease, accidents, and other fateful incidents. He cannot escape death and he is subject to the winds of fortune.

In the anxiety of emptiness and meaninglessness, belief breaks down through external or internal events. One feels cut off from creative participation in spheres of culture and one is driven from one devotion to another.

In the anxiety of guilt and condemnation, man feels the demand to become what he is meant to become, but at the same time he realizes that his best deed does not fulfill his potentialities. Hence, he feels guilty.

Tillich contends that these are essential anxieties; i.e., they are inevitable, a part of man's existence. He must live with them. As essential, they are distinguished from the distortions that occur because man is not able to live with them. These distortions are the pathological anxieties in which one's anxiety (1) is turned into fear of leaving security or into feelings of security when one is not safe, (2) takes the form of striving for a narrow castle of certitude that becomes fanaticism, or takes the form of misplaced doubt, and (3) is met by reducing decisions to a minimum in order to avoid guilt or by feeling guilty when there is no reason for guilt.

This description of anxiety has been included in order to indicate that a description of what man is meant to be includes his participation in the essential anxieties, but not in the distortions.

However, Tillich claims that although we know much about man through reason and experience, what man is meant to be can be known ultimately only in the picture of Jesus as the Christ. Here we find what Tillich calls the catholic substance (love) and the protestant principle (the denial of an absolute status to any embodiment of love). These two elements give general content to the *Image of God*. Furthermore, since Tillich defines that Kingdom of God as "individual fulfillment within universal fulfillment," the presence of the *Image of God* in man cannot be conceived as something possessed by an individual in his solitude.

Emil Brunner provides us with one of the most extensive recent discussions of the Christian doctrine of man in his *Man in Revolt*. He insists that the *Image of God* does not refer to something which a man can possess as he possesses reason. What distinguishes man from other creatures can be known only by reflecting on what Jesus Christ tells us about ourselves. There we discover that being in the *Image of God* means, in the first place, the acceptance of our being a creature, dependent upon God's continual sustaining activity. Thus, man cannot be man by himself. He is man only as related to the divine Being who creates and sustains him. Furthermore, since this Divine Being stands in a similar relation to many men, man is not "man" except he share this relation of community. Man cannot escape this given situation, although he tries to reject it. In the second place, in becoming what he is meant to be (i.e., in being truly human), one accepts his creaturely dependent status and re-ponds to the continuing activity of God as requiring responsible action on his part. This action takes the form of furthering the "union of human beings in love." Thus, the being and worth of a man does not reside in himself, but in God who continually confronts him, asking for a decision in favor of responsible existence.

Brunner emphasizes the difficulty in attributing historical status to the truth pointed to by Adam and original righteousness. He feels that to conceive of the *Image of God* as present in Adam in a primitive state in the past, is to fail to deal seriously with our own creation in the *Image of God*.

In the theology of Karl Barth [12] we find one of the most

---

[12] All the material on Barth is dependent on Otto Weber, *Karl Barth's Church Dogmatics,* translated by Arthur Cochrane (London: Lutterworth, 1953).

provocative of modern biblical theological discussions of man. Here, too, we look to Jesus Christ to find the character of the human nature God has made. There we find what we "are," although Jesus does not do what we do. Although he is tempted, he holds his ground and thus reveals what human nature is created to be. The question of how his peculiar status as Son of God affects his human nature is not clear. Barth, in keeping with the classical Christian position, must reject the notion that his constitution is different, lest he give up the humanness of Jesus and all that is implied by his two natures. Were we to depend upon man as known in ordinary experience and the sciences, we could know only what man has made of man. Were not Jesus at once man and "more than man," we could not know more from him than from any man.

When we look to the man Jesus to find the real nature of man, we find that Jesus is (1) the man for God, (2) the man for other men, (3) the whole man, and (4) the Lord of time. Hence, the real man is (1) God's creature, (2) God's covenant partner, (3) an ordered unity of soul and body, and (4) destined to "fall asleep" without dying in judgment. There is, then, a parallel between the nature of Jesus and that of man.

As God's creature, the real man is man as elected. It is the intention of the Creator that man be victorious. Again, to be a creature for God is to exist in that sphere of the creaturely world in which God's Word is uttered and becomes known. Finally, as God's creature, man is a history rather than a "state."

Thus, as man acquires an "existence in the history founded by Jesus" he is a real man. To be man means to be preserved by God's mercy for Jesus' sake and to adhere to God's righteousness for Jesus' sake. Thus, real human existence from God's side is existence in gratitude, in thanksgiving; from man's side it is defined as responsibility. In this responsibility man possesses the character of knowledge of God, of obedience to God, of invocation to God, and of freedom given by God.

As God's covenant partner the real man is made for other men. This is not something added to man's existence. It is like the relation in God's own inner divine being. Man's existence, then, involves encounter in which (1) one deals with every other as a distinct individual rather than as a member of a group, (2) there is listening to and speaking to the other, (3) there is mutual aid, and (4) the give and take occurs gladly as if one were unable to do otherwise. This cohumanity (existence in community) of man finds exemplification in the Genesis account of the creation of man as male and female. There we find the basis for the conviction that no man alone embodies the *Image of God*. It is only in their togetherness, as two, as male and female, or as more than one, that man exists in the *Image of God*.

As an ordered unity of soul and body, the real man has spirit, but he is not spirit. The possession of or by the spirit designates an action and attitude of the Creator with respect to his creature. This spirit is not only in the "new" man, but is the "principle" of man's creatureliness. Thus, neither the soul as the animation of the body, nor the body as related to the activity of the soul, is the source of man's creaturely status. Furthermore, soul and body are integrally related. Man is an ordered unity because he receives in God's Word that which makes him a man.

As destined to fall asleep without "dying in judgment," the real man is described as one who can have a "true and proper existence in time." My "now" is, therefore, accepted as the now prepared by God for *me*, and my past is accepted as *my* past. Therefore, man may either remember it with gratitude or forget it in God's name. Similarly, we may look forward to the future as time that is in God's hands. Man is finite. He exists as one with a time that begins and ends. But the beginning is not an abyss but from Jesus Christ, from the God revealed in Jesus Christ. The end brings death or the falling asleep (non-existence), but the second death, the dying in judgment, does not belong to "man's nature created by God and therefore to his good nature."

V. THE IMAGE OF GOD IN MAN: CONCLUSIONS

We have presented, thus far, material from (1) the Old and New Testaments, (2) representative theologians influential in the history of the church, (3) modern secular thought, and (4) modern theologians. It may seem unnecessary to work through some of these materials either in their brief presentations here or in the more extended discussions in the original sources. It is our conviction, however, that the best way to guard against shallow and uncritical views of the Christian faith is to confront the Scriptures and the developing tradition frequently, and to compare it with modern thought and practice, both secular and Christian. Now, however, we must state briefly what conclusions we reach after this exploration.

We shall attempt to present what we consider to be a position rooted in the Bible, for we hold that what man is meant to be is disclosed in Jesus Christ. But the full meaning of Jesus as the Christ is known only as the New Testament picture of Christ is understood in the light of (1) the history of the people who first accepted him as Christ, (2) their experiences of renewal through faith, and (3) experience of the faithful down through the generations.

The Old Testament picture of the creation of man suggests two important aspects of man's essential nature. First, since man is created in the *Image of God,* we assume the act of creation. Man is more than "a noble animal, splendid in ashes and pompous in the grave." [13] As created, man becomes a part of God's purpose. Second, as created in the *Image of God* as good, man is given the opportunity to achieve God's purpose. Christ served God's purpose that the world might be reconciled to God. Men have been created with hearts that are restless until they find rest in Him who is the source and fountain of their being. Man is made for God. Everything that man is and does is real when it glorifies God. As creatures, men find their meaning and purpose not primarily in their own existence, but in serving him who created them and thus that for which they were created. Practically, this means that man turns away from himself to find his meaning. He finds it in God's intention for him.

The New Testament discussion of the image indicates to us that since we see now only in a mirror dimly, we must look to Christ to discover God's intention. This does not mean that we can know nothing about what we are intended to be by looking at man himself. Certainly men are not made to become mentally ill. Men are not made to tear themselves and others apart by virtue of their anxieties. Men are not meant to treat each other as tools, as pawns in a struggle for power. There is much that we can learn about what man is meant to be or not meant to be, by looking at what man has made of man. But a million looks are not sufficient if we turn only to man, since man as we know him is not good. There is none good save God, and we find what goodness is when we find God. Thus God's activity becomes the gate through which we find the good. God's activity in the Christ of history is the entrance. This activity has a creative and redemptive function. Man knows God's intention for him in a general way through Christ's revelation of man's created nature. He knows God's intention for him in a specific way

---

[13] From "Hydriotaphia" (Urn Burial), by Thomas Browne; published by Joseph Rickerby, Sherbourne Lane, London, 1838.

through his knowledge of God's purpose as disclosed in his own experience as a "new" creature. We know that we are meant to glorify God since Jesus the man stands firm in that direction, saying "not what I will, but what thou wilt." We know that we are meant to glorify God because only in those moments when we are free to glorify him does our restlessness cease.

Thus, the *Image of God* is both (1) something we can point to, God in Christ Jesus, and (2) man's turning to God, something that depends upon God's call and man's responsible answer in each moment.

This general pattern and purpose, obedience to God's will and the glorification of God, suggests that this is not something man possesses as he possesses the capacity for speech. What man is created to be must always be seen in relation to God's intention and will. The response to the creative activity of God at any moment provides the concrete content of the *Image of God*.

But there is more that can be said about the content of the *Image of God*. One may seek to derive man's existence in community from the creation of man as male and female, from God's covenant relation with his people, from Christ's relation to his congregation, or from the facts of our dependence upon the other for our existence as real persons. In each case we learn that man is not man alone. He truly is man only in community; i.e., where there are bonds of mutual support, affection, judgment, and forgiveness. The *Image of God*, therefore, is not something one individual can possess. It can be present only in relationships involving man with God and man with his fellow creatures. It can be known and realized only where the community of faith and love (the church) nourish and sustain the man of faith.

Thus far we have stated very formal aspects of man's essential being: (1) his purpose—to obey and to glorify God, and (2) his being—an individual in community. Let us press on to ask whether or not rationality, freedom, finitude, rule over things, responsibility, and concern for the neighbor are elements of man's essential nature or activity. We find it necessary to include these aspects of man's life. We include them because they do not represent to us aspects of man's existence due to sin. But they are not of equal importance. To say that man is finite indicates that man must die. He is mortal. But this does not mean that man is created to die the "death of judgment" referred to in the discussion of Barth. To say that essential man is rational says a great deal, but it is not so important to man as his existence as a responsible servant of the neighbor. Thus we are led to reject the location of the image in a special part of the person. The image is related to the whole man.

Finally, we affirm that the *Image of God,* designating man's essential nature, does not find its role chiefly in defining an original state of righteousness or in describing man as he will be when all things will be "new." The *Image of God* points to man as he is meant to be. It designates what man, in some measure can be, through God's redeeming action in Christ. Therefore, "Put off your old nature which belongs to your former manner of life and is corrupt through deceitful lusts, and be renewed in the spirit of your minds, and put on the new nature, created after the likeness of God in true righteousness and holiness" (Eph. 4:22-24).

BIBLIOGRAPHY

Brunner, Emil, *Man in Revolt.* New York: Charles Scribner's Sons, 1939, 564 pp.

Cairns, David, *The Image of God in Man.* New York: Philosophical Library, 1953, 255 pp.

Eichrodt, Walter, *Man in the Old Testament.* Chicago: H. Regnery Co., 1951, 83 pp.

Hamilton, William, *The Christian Man*. Philadelphia: Westminster Press, 1956, 93 pp.

Niebuhr, Reinhold, *The Nature and Destiny of Man*. New York: Charles Scribner's Sons, 1945, 2 Vols.

Tillich, Paul, *The Courage to Be*. New Haven: Yale University Press, 1952, 185 pp.

Torrance, Thomas F., *Calvin's Doctrine of Man*. London: Lutterworth Press, 1949, 183 pp.

Weber, Otto, *Karl Barth's Church Dogmatics*. Translated by Arthur C. Cochrane, Philadelphia: Westminster Press, 1953, 253 pp.

Wright, George Ernest, *The Biblical Doctrine of Man in Society*. London: SCM Press, 1954, 176 pp.

V

HOW GOD OVERCOMES SIN:
ATONEMENT AND JUSTIFICATION

ROBERT T. HANDY

I. HISTORICAL

PAUL, EXPLAINING to the Corinthians what was "of first importance" in the gospel he had received, began his enumeration by saying "Christ died for our sins in accordance with the scriptures" (1 Cor. 15:3). Christian men and women from the first to the twentieth century have sought to understand more clearly what it means to say this. They have continually examined the relevant biblical passages that they might have a fuller understanding of the meaning of the atonement.

When we try to understand the atonement today, we should remember that we do not start *de novo*. John Knox has recently reminded us that one cannot go back to the first century except by way of the second: "No body of Christians actually 'skips or by-passes the second century' and returns directly and freshly to the first." [1] It is no less true that we cannot get back to the first century except through the other centuries—we are also heirs of the eleventh, the sixteenth, and the nineteenth centuries, for example. In those centuries various ways of understanding the atonement were developed. Consciously or unconsciously, directly or indirectly, they tend to influence our thinking as we search the Scriptures for ourselves.

Historical attempts to frame an adequate doctrine of the atonement have been necessary and helpful. But the very richness and variety of the biblical material on which these efforts have been built had led to difficulties. A specific attempt to frame a doctrine of the atonement may easily overemphasize certain things and neglect others. Proponents of a particular position, however, have been prone to claim that their view preserves the fullness of gospel teaching. This has caused others to react sharply and to frame their own view in part against what they felt was a distortion. Thus, the major ways of understanding have been shaped not only by the New Testament but also by each other.

Furthermore, the various attempts to present a doctrine of the atonement have inevitably been influenced by the cultural, political, and intellectual atmosphere of the times in which they were articulated.[2] Therefore, the accidents of history have played some part in man's effort to understand how Christ died for our sins; and we can learn much from the theologians of the past, both by seeking to be informed

[1] From *The Early Church and the Coming Great Church,* p. 139, by John Knox; copyright, 1955, Abingdon Press, New York.

[2] Shailer Mathews has made this unforgettably clear in the *The Atonement and the Social Process* (New York: Macmillan Co., 1930). His insistence on the importance of historical contexts can be accepted without agreeing with his assumption that because analogical elements are present in a doctrinal expression it is therefore somehow no longer significant, nor assenting to his sharp separation of religious experience and theological belief.

by their genuine insights and by striving to avoid their distortions. We should also be reminded that our own attempts to frame an adequate doctrine of the atonement will be limited by the particular age in which we live.

Though there have been many different attempts to frame a doctrine of the atonement adequate to the revelation of God in Christ, it is possible to see them as falling into several main lines of interpretation. Usually three such general types are mentioned, although they are often explained in somewhat different fashion. The New Testament has usually been read in the light of one of them. It may be that each approach has caught in a distinctive way facets of the gospel which are essential to its full understanding. Efforts to delineate these three main lines in too narrow or too rigid patterns will distort rather than clarify the history of the doctrine. But there do appear to have been three major types of doctrine of the atonement; and these main approaches have been very influential, though there are also minor patterns, and sometimes a given statement will be influenced by more than one type.

The *"classic," "ransom," or "dramatic"* theories of the atonement were set forth in the early centuries and long dominated the field. The position was clearly delineated by Irenaeus and developed in various ways by theologians like Athanasius, Augustine, and Gregory the Great. It was predicated on the belief that Jesus Christ is the Word of God incarnate, that God himself in Christ entered into the world of sin and death so that he might overcome the powers that hold men in bondage, and reconcile the world to himself. The position assumed a dualistic context in which the work of Christ was done—the forces of evil were seen to have posed a real threat to the divine will, and were overcome by a real struggle.

According to this understanding, men were enslaved by

the efforts of Satan, who had tempted them successfully and enticed them into bondage. Christ contended with all the powers of evil and emerged triumphant; he decisively defeated them and broke their grip over men.

Irenaeus used the image of ransom freely in explaining his views, regarding it as having been paid to the powers of evil. Through this ransom the evil forces have been overcome and their hold over men brought to an end. The resurrection proved that Christ was supreme over death and the devil; therefore reconciliation was effected, and a new relationship between God and man made possible through Christ. In a word, Christ furnished man with salvation; what had been lost in Adam was recovered in Christ. Immortality and communion with God are possible because of what has been done in the work of Christ.

For many centuries, discussion of the atonement was in this "classic" context—now crudely, now more cautiously expounded. Whatever its weaknesses (e.g., the dubious premise that Satan must be bought off by God, and the development of the position by men like Gregory the Great to the extent of saying that Satan was "baited" by Christ), it emphasized that the work of atonement stems from divine initiative and grace, and insisted that through Christ came the victory of life over death and good over evil. This general approach dominated the field until it was challenged in the eleventh century by the other two major types. It has continued to influence Christian theology, and has been put forth in our day by some influential theologians—Aulen especially has stressed this line of thought, though he has minimized the "ransom" and emphasized the dramatic and dualistic features of the position.[3]

The classic position was sharply challenged by Anselm of

---

[3] Gustaf Aulen, *Christus Victor* (London: S.P.C.K., 1931).

Canterbury, who developed the *"satisfaction," "objective," or "juridical"* position. He did not believe that the devil had any power over death and could not see why any ransom had to be paid to him. What man does need is redemption from sin. Sin is any act on the part of man depriving God of the honor due to him; it is rebellion against God, defiance of the divine majesty, violation of the divine honor. God cannot forgive man by disregarding his sin, for then he would be letting sin go unpunished, and would himself be immoral. Divine justice requires either eternal punishment for the rebellion against the eternal God, or an infinite satisfaction that the honor of the Infinite be upheld. But man, corrupted by the fall, cannot make the necessary payment. Only a God-man could offer the requisite infinite satisfaction; only he who was sinless and did not have to die could render that which was required, by giving himself voluntarily. The death of the Incarnate, the God-man, Christ, was of infinite value, and so its benefits are transferable to men. Therefore, God became man so that the God-man by his death might pay the satisfaction for the sin of men.

This approach became normative for medieval theology. Doctrines advanced by particular theologians varied in detail, but the overall pattern largely replaced the classic, ransom theories. Aquinas' modifications of the Anselmic approach became especially influential. Protestant atonement doctrine also tended to be shaped largely by this understanding. Luther, to be sure, combined certain aspects of ransom theory with objective motifs—Aulen attempts to show that the classic elements were indeed dominant in Luther's position. But most orthodox Protestant thought took the satisfaction position. The "penal theory" spread swiftly in Protestant circles; according to it, Christ's death was understood as the satisfaction rendered for sin. Anselm had distinguished between satisfaction and punishment, but the Reformers, treating sin as a violation of the divine justice, understood the satisfaction as the actual punishment accepted by Christ.

Another modification of the objective theory, which was popular especially in certain Calvinistic circles, was the "governmental theory" explicated by Grotius. This position assumed the necessity of an "antecedent satisfaction" as a condition for forgiveness, but defined it as the punishment accepted by Christ in order to provide an example of the penalty which sin deserves and to uphold the sovereignty of the divine law. Men could thus see the terribleness of their sinful situation, yet they also could be recipients of the divine forgiveness because the majesty of the law had been upheld by Christ's voluntary sacrifice.

Pietistic Protestantism has tended to emphasize a simplified version of the satisfaction approach—the substitutionary view. Christ died for our sins upon the cross; in the spirit of self-sacrifice he took our place and suffered for us what we deserve, thereby lifting the burden from us if we will receive him in faith.

Today, theories of the atonement according to the objective approach have their strong proponents. For example, Emil Brunner has gone back to Anselm himself in developing his doctrine of the atonement.

The third major type was proposed and developed vigorously by Anselm's younger contemporary Abelard, and is known as the *"subjective," "moral (influence)," or "experiential"* view. Abelard emphasized strongly God's sovereignty —he believed in predestination—and argued that God was bound by no necessity, but could save men in any way he might please. But inasmuch as his nature is love, he would not be pleased, Abelard insisted, by the death of an innocent man. And how, he asked, could the value of Christ's death be transferred to others? No, Christ the incarnate Son of God permitted himself to be crucified to make evident the unfathomable depths of God's love, for God was willing to see his Son suffer to make clear to men the terribleness of their sin and the great distance he would go to recall them. From the cross, he who said "Father, forgive them," showed the fullness of the forgiving nature of God. Contemplation of the divine love, so unforgettably dramatized on the cross, drives men to repentance and sends them forth to seek a life of sacrifice like his.

In medieval times this approach did not have a large following, though its emphasis on the change in men effected by the atonement was accepted by Aquinas and others and grafted onto the dominant objective position. The fruits, but not the roots of the type, were thus appropriated. It was not until recent centuries, and especially in modern Protestantism, that the Abelardian position has become central, though most often set in an Arminian, Socinian, or liberal theological framework. The theological tradition stemming from Schleiermacher has often presented some form of this theory. Horace Bushnell combined both objective and subjective themes in his theological writing, but it was the subjective emphasis which was seized on by his followers and which became an important force in American preaching.

To try to press this over-all three-fold analysis too far will lead to distortion. As useful an effort as Aulen's does not escape this. Doctrines of the atonement which do not readily fit into any of the approaches have been influential; doctrines which carry the stamp of more than one line of thought have had their followers. We may see a fourth major pattern emerge presently—indeed, an approach focusing on the themes of "sacrifice" and "expiation" is now being advanced. Vincent Taylor shows how the sacrificial approach, which has deep Old Testament roots and which has been tangentially influential throughout the history of the doctrine, has not yet been comprehensively worked out, though he himself has made a sustained and rigorous effort to do so in his writings.[4]

In Baptist circles, there has been great diversity as to atonement doctrine. In the original Calvinistic context, both penal and governmental theories were familiar. With the spread of pietism, the substitutionary position became almost standard. As liberalism emerged from evangelicalism, the emphasis was shifted to moral influence doctrines. Today, the theological renaissance has inclined many Baptists to seek an understanding of the atonement which will retain both objective and subjective emphases; there is an openness to creative thought based on all classical types.

II. BIBLICAL

"If we come to the New Testament expecting to find a cut-and-dried theory of the rationale of the atonement, we shall be disappointed," writes F. W. Dillistone.[5] "No theory of the Atonement is presented in the New Testament, but the material upon which theories are based is present in great abundance," affirms Vincent Taylor.[6] The New Testament is truly rich in the variety of language used to describe the significance of the death and resurrection of Christ. A multiplicity of themes are suggested. This very fullness is inspiring, but very baffling as we try to state what the atonement means to us. The richness of the biblical imagery is in a way suggestive of its quality of divinity, for in none but a profusion of motifs and pictures could the meaning of the

---

[4] Cf. his *The Atonement in New Testament Teaching* (2nd ed.; London: Epworth Press, 1945), esp. pp. 186-88, and his *Forgiveness and Reconciliation* (2nd ed.; London: Macmillan Co., 1946), pp. 182 f.

[5] From *The Significance of the Cross*, p. 35, by F. W. Dillistone; copyright, 1944, The Westminster Press. Used by permission.

[6] From *The Atonement in New Testament Teaching*, pp. 182f., by Vincent Taylor; The Epworth Press, 1945.

person and work of the Son of the infinite and eternal God even be suggested to us. In none but a complex tapestry of themes and images could the mystery of the crucified and risen Lord be made available to us. If we can at once learn from the historical approaches to the understanding of the atonement and yet break through them, the New Testament may speak to us anew, suggesting fresh, broad, and deep meanings of what Christ has done for us.

We can find that there are at least half a dozen significant themes in the New Testament, all of which are relevant to an understanding of the atonement, though they may vary in original emphasis and present importance. Two themes occur so generally throughout the New Testament, and in such important passages, that it is natural to begin with them.[7]

One of the most frequent ways of describing the atonement in the New Testament is found in the group of terms that refer to it as *redemption*. The word most commonly used in Paul and in the rest of the New Testament is *apolutrōsis* (cf., e.g., Rom. 3:24; 1 Cor. 1:30; Eph. 1:7; Col. 1:14; Heb. 9:15). This word contains the root *lutr-*, which denotes the price paid (ransom) to emancipate a slave. This is a direct carryover from two Hebrew words for redemption, both of which expressed the idea of buying something back or paying a price to secure a benefit.

Direct use of the word "ransom" (*lutron*) is found in the New Testament only in Jesus' saying that he came "to give his life as a ransom for many" (Mark 10:45; Matt. 20:28) and in Paul's word that Christ "gave himself as a ranson [*anti-lutron*] for all" (1 Tim. 2:6). The verb "to ransom" (*lutroō*) is used in Titus 2:14 and 1 Peter 1:18f., but there is no question raised here about who received the ransom; the emphasis is on the fact that all benefit from this redemption.

---

[7] The word-study on which this section is largely based is adapted from an extensive preliminary paper by George D. Younger.

It is in the more general form of "redemption" (*apolutrō-sis*) that this root occurs in Paul and in the rest of the New Testament. Knowing that the Greek root *lutr-* refers to the ransom paid to emancipate a slave, expositors have been tempted to read the idea of "ransom" into every passage where *apolutrōsis* is used. But even the two Hebrew words for redemption had long before lost their specific character and were used in a general way in the Old Testament to refer to God's deliverance of Israel (Deut. 7:8; Isa. 43:1; 51:11). Paul and his readers were familiar with this use of *apolutrōsis* as "deliverance;" indeed, it is used this way in the Septuagint. Hence it is better to understand the New Testament use of "redemption" in terms of Israel's deliverance from slavery in Egypt and deliverance from exile in Babylon rather than the more individualistic picture of the emancipation of a Greek or Roman slave.

There is another group of words used to express the idea of redemption. They have the common root *agor-*, which refers to a purchase made in the marketplace (*agora*). One verb in this group usually means "to buy" (*agorazō*); it is used in 1 Cor. 6:20; 7:23; 2 Pet. 2:1; Rev. 5:9; 14:3-5. Another form of the word, *exagorazō*, is translated "to redeem" in Gal. 3:13, and 4:5f. Although the idea of purchase is in the background, there is no reference to a recipient of any purchase money, and the more general idea of redemption comes to the fore.

Thus the idea that Christ gave his life to redeem us clearly runs through the New Testament. The underlying images—a ransom to free a slave, the deliverance of Israel from bondage, a purchase in the market-place—are at no point developed or clarified. The words seem to have been used in a generalized or abstract way, far from their points of origin.

The theme of *sacrifice* is another which is widely used in connection with the idea of atonement in the New Testament, and in varying contexts. One sacrificial idea which appears very early is the interpretation of Christ's death as the *covenant-sacrifice* which seals the New Covenant. The passages which refer to the institution of the Lord's Supper (cf. 1 Cor. 11:25; Luke 22:19; Matt. 26:28) all emphasize this. According to Mark 14:24, Jesus said, "This is my blood of the covenant, which is poured out for many." The meaning is clear: as the "blood of the covenant" which Moses threw over the altar and over the people at Sinai sealed the covenant with Israel (Ex. 24:4-8), so the pouring out of the blood of Christ in death, as symbolized by the cup, is the sign of the new covenant between God and his people. The new covenant is referred to many times in Hebrews (cf. 7:22; 8:6,13; 9:15; 12:24), including several references to the "blood of the covenant" (cf. Heb. 9:20; 10:29; 13:20).

Jesus was identified at a very early date with the Suffering Servant of Isa. 53, who offers himself as a guilt-offering (*asham*) for the sins of others. The apostolic sermons in Acts (3:13; 4:27,30) contain references that suggest this figure of prophecy. The characteristic name for Christ in these passages is *pais* (also used in the Septuagint translation of Isa. 53), which is best rendered into English as "servant." Acts 8:26-35 shows Philip using Isa. 53:7f. as a starting-point to tell "the good news of Jesus" to the Ethiopian eunuch. And some find suggestions of the Servant in Jesus' own statement of Mark 10:45 and Matt. 20:28.

Although the use of sacrificial language and imagery is limited in the Gospels and in Acts, it is much more frequent in Paul, whose Epistles used the very words "sacrifice" (*thusia*) and "to sacrifice" (*thuō*) several times. 1 Cor. 5:7 declares that "Christ, our paschal lamb, has been sacrificed." Eph. 5:2 asks the church to "walk in love, as Christ loved us and gave himself up for us, a fragrant offering and sacrifice to God." The reference is to the Old Testament burnt

offerings where the smoke ascending from the altar was supposed to be pleasing to God. It ought to be added that Paul
did not reserve the idea of sacrifice for the death of Christ
(cf. 2 Cor. 2:15; Phil. 2:17; 4:18; 2 Tim. 4:6).

Pauline writings several times use the word "blood" to
refer to Christ's life being poured out on the cross (cf. Rom.
5:9; Eph. 1:7; 2:13; Col. 1:20). In these passages, where the
main reference is to other atonement themes, it is fair to
assume that "blood" is used as an equivalent for Christ's
death, because the efficacy of a sacrifice was the life force
(blood of the victim) set free through death so that it might
be effective for others. In Rom. 3:25 the word appears more
clearly in the context of sacrifice; Paul speaks of Christ Jesus,
"whom God put forward as an expiation [*hilastērion*] by his
blood." Words with *hilas-* as their root used to be translated
"propitiation," suggesting the idea of appeasement of God
through an offering. But biblical scholarship has found that
the use of *hilastērion* in the Septuagint clearly favors "expiation" as the proper translation, and the Revised Standard
Version follows this usage. This suggests that when Paul
spoke of the blood of Christ he was thinking of it as "cover-
ing" mans sin, annulling sin and its effects, rather than ap-
peasing the wrath of God. The First Epistle of John also
makes use of this concept of expiation (*hilasmos*) which
cleanses us from sin or blots it out (cf. 1 John 2:2; 4:10).

The Revelation to John makes use of sacrificial concepts
in presenting the eternal significance of the death of Christ.
In the context of the allegory, the risen Christ is the "Lamb
standing, as though it had been slain" (Rev. 5:6), still bearing
the marks of sacrifice. "The blood of the Lamb" is the phrase
often used in the Apocalypse to refer to the atonement which
frees, redeems, and purifies us (cf. Rev. 1:5; 5:9; 7:14; 14:3-5).

The Letter to the Hebrews makes greater use of the language of sacrifice than any other New Testament book; a sustained sacrificial comparison is utilized to emphasize the uniqueness and finality of Christ's atonement. The main picture evoked by the sacrificial passages in Hebrews is the Day of Atonement (cf. Lev. 16), when sin offerings and burnt offerings were presented for the sins committed unwittingly during the previous year by the priests and by the people. Hebrews compares and contrasts the sin offering on the Day of Atonement and Christ's death: the former could not atone for deliberate sin, while Christ atoned for all sins (cf. Heb. 9:12-14; 10:1-18); the former sacrifice was offered in a sanctuary made with hands, while Christ's was offered in the heavenly original of the sanctuary. Christ's sacrificial work of atonement brings purification for sins, redemption, clear conscience, sanctification, and perfection (cf. Heb. 1:3; 9:12, 26; 10:10,14). Thus Hebrews refers to the blood of Jesus both as the new and better sacrifice after the pattern of the Day of Atonement, and also as the "covenant-blood" after the pattern of Exodus.

It is clear that the theme of sacrifice is found in many places in the New Testament. But we need to heed the warning of Vincent Taylor—whose contemporary effort to understand the atonement in terms of sacrifice makes his words all the more emphatic at this point—who insists that the use of sacrificial terms and pictures by New Testament writers is not to be understood at all as a literal acceptance of the sacrificial system of the Temple. After careful study of the evidence, he has concluded:

> These facts suggest that the true significance of the sacrificial element undeniably present in New Testament teaching is to be found not so much in the specific rites of the cultus, as in the underlying ideas of sacrifice, the idea of the drawing near of the worshiper to God in humility and contrition, the thought of an offering with which he can iden-

tify himself in penitence and faith, the conception of sharing in the cleansing power of life which has been released in death, dedicated, and presented to God.[8]

We turn next to two themes which are central to the message of Paul, though they are not found generally in the rest of the New Testament. Their depth of insight has commended them to Christians seeking to understand the meaning of the cross through the centuries.

The first of these is *reconciliation*. This emphasis may be implied in the synoptic accounts of the rending of the curtain of the temple at the hour of Jesus' death (cf. Mark 15:38; Matt. 27:51; Luke 23:45), which give a vivid picture of the new relation between God and man made possible thereby (cf. also Heb. 9:8; 10:19f.). But it is Paul who specifically used the word "reconciliation" (*katallagē*, translated "atonement" in the King James Version) and the two verbs which mean "to reconcile" (*katalassō, apokatalassō*). The underlying picture in this motif is of estrangement or hostility between two persons or groups which is put away by a decisive act. The root meaning of the Greek words is that of an exchange of equivalent values producing a radical change (cf. Rom. 5:10f.; 2 Cor. 5:18-21).

Paul often conjoins the idea of reconciliation with another theme which has deep Old Testament connotations, that of "peace" (*shalom*). *Shalom,* in the Old Testament, carries the connotation of "well-being" and "harmony," not only among men and nations but also with God and his whole creation. (Cf. Rom. 15:33; 16:20; Gal. 1:19-22; 2:13-17; Eph. 6:15; 2 Thess. 3:16; cf. also Heb. 13:20, the only place outside of Paul where atonement is directly related to peace.) Paul speaks of Jesus Christ as mediator (*mesitēs*), or intercessor between God and man (1 Tim. 2:5f.); a different word (*para-*

---

[8] Taylor, *op. cit.*, p. 187.

clētos), but with a similar meaning, is to be found in 1 John 2:1.

The other theme which is chiefly Pauline is that of *justification*. Bible commentators generally agree that in the original languages of both testaments the words "justification" and "righteousness" rest on the same root, both linguistically and doctrinally. The single Greek word *dikaios* is usually rendered as either "just" or "righteous" in our New Testament translations. The words which express the idea of justification have a common root (*dik-*) and include such words as *dikaiōma* (a declaration of right), *dikaiōsis* (a setting right), and *dikaioō* (to make or declare right, to justify). Paul, of course, had become convinced that the law, the Jewish instrument of righteousness, could not free a man from sin; it could not justify him. In this context he insisted that it was because of Christ's death, the benefits of which could be appropriated by faith, that justification was possible. Righteousness for man does not reside essentially in the horizontal dimension, it resides rather in the vertical dimension (cf. Rom. 1:17). *Dikaiōsis* comes near to being a normative expression for justification, obtainable by faith (cf. Rom. 4:24f.; 5:1,18f.).

The usage of *dikaioō* is crucial, for here we come to grips with the way man is made right. Clearly, justification in the New Testament has definite, inescapable behavioral connotations: for example, see Matt. 12:34b-37 (v.37 has the word *dikaioō*), Rom. 2:13; James 2:18-26; Rev. 19:8. But the crucial issue is how a man realizes upright relationships with God: does he by his righteousness so stand that God "declares" him justified, or is he through faith "made" just, that is, set on the path of righteous living as a consequence of his faith? Though the declarative aspect can be argued from the New Testament (as in the passages above), the second emphasis seems to us to be the proper one.

The lawyer referred to in Luke 10 was probably thinking of the first emphasis when he asked Jesus about eternal life. When the issue was defined in terms of love of God and neighbor, "he, desiring to *justify* himself, said to Jesus, 'And who is my neighbor?' " (Luke 10:29). Here is exhibited man's tendency to declare himself right (*dikaioō*) as he is, and, in consequence, to be declared righteous by God almost as an earned right. But Jesus was constantly countering this tendency: "But he said to them [the Pharisees], 'You are those who justify yourselves before men, but God knows your hearts' " (Luke 16:15). The inner orientation of the man is the crux of the matter, as Jesus made clear in his comment on the Pharisee and the publican: "I tell you, this man went down to his house justified [*dikaioō*] rather than the other; for every one who exalts himself will be humbled, but he who humbles himself will be exalted" (Luke 18:14).

Paul customarily uses *dikaioō* in the sense of "to make right"; for him justification is decidedly through grace by faith (cf. Rom. 3:20-25; Gal. 2:16; 3:24). In one place outside of Paul's writings the language of justification is used directly in connection with the atonement (cf. 1 Pet. 2:24; 3:18); here it is linked to the theme of reconciliation also. Basically, the New Testament insists that righteousness as a personal, ethical character follows upon a fundamental inner reorientation of life which stems from grace and faith, and not vice versa (cf., e.g., Rom. 8:10; Phil. 3:9; 1 Pet. 2:24).

We turn now to two themes concerning the atonement which are of minor importance in terms of New Testament emphasis, although they have received much attention in later theological thinking. The theme of *deliverance* or rescue (closely related, of course, to our first theme of redemption) can be found in Paul and Revelation. *Apolutrōsis,* as has been noted, can mean both redemption and deliverance. But Paul also used *ruomai,* "to deliver," or "to rescue," in connection with the atonement (cf. Gal. 1:4; Col. 1:13 f; 1 Thess. 1:10). The various words having the meaning of "save" reinforce this usage (Eph. 5:23; Phil. 3:20; 1 Tim. 1:15; 2 Tim. 1:10). The Revelation to John, in using the verb *luō*, to free, suggests the idea of deliverance from an enemy (cf. e.g., Rev. 1:5).

The theme of the *overthrow of hostile powers* is linked to the atonement by Paul in the letter to the Colossians (cf. 2:15; 1:13). The underlying picture is that of a conquering king who, having defeated the "principalities and powers" (cf. Rom. 8:38; Eph. 3:10) on a battlefield, disarms them, and, like a Roman conqueror, leads them in triumph in a public procession. The theme of the overcoming of hostile powers—in this case, the devil—is reflected also in 1 John 3:8, and in Rev. 12:10 f.

These are the most important themes used in the New Testament to describe and explain the atonement. Others do occur, especially in Paul's writings. For example, there are the themes of cancelled debt (cf. Col. 2:14), of adoption (cf. Rom. 8:14-17; Gal. 4:1-7), and of self-emptying, *kenōsis*, (cf. 2 Cor. 8:9; Phil. 2:5-11). These, however, do not receive the attention or development the major themes that have been discussed do.

The Fourth Gospel in referring to the atonement speaks of the way the Father has "glorified," *doxazō*, (cf. John 7:39; 12:16,23; 13:31 f., 17:1) and "lifted up," *hupsoō* (cf. John 3:14; 8:28; 12:32) his Son so that eternal life will be available to men.

It must be strongly emphasized that often a number of these themes are woven together in a single passage. To pick an example:

> For there is no distinction; since all have sinned and fall short of the glory of God, they are justified by his grace as a gift, through the redemption which is in Christ Jesus, whom

> God put forward as an expiation by his blood, to be re-
> ceived by faith. This was to show God's righteousness, be-
> cause in his divine forbearance he had passed over former
> sins; it was to prove at the present time that he himself is
> righteous and that he justifies him who has faith in Jesus
> (Rom. 3:22b-26).

Here the themes of redemption, sacrifice, and justification
are combined; many other passages also show the commin-
gling of various themes. One theme may serve to deepen our
understanding of others. But strict logic is not enough to
deal with the subtle depths of the New Testament statements about the atonement. The flood of imagery found in
its pages should not be asked to stand merely literal analysis,
for all these various themes point beyond themselves to
Christ himself and his work.

III. THEOLOGICAL

This brief analysis of the New Testament material on atonement makes it quite clear that none of the main historical
approaches to the understanding of the atonement is fully
adequate. One of the pressing theological tasks of our time
is the setting forth of a new synthesis which will bring the
atonement more vividly and meaningfully to the mind of
modern man. This doctrine will need to be larger than anything that has yet caught the imagination of the church, for
the various New Testament themes converge at a number of
points to declare what would seem to be the essential ingredi-
ents of a full doctrine of the atonement. We suggest that
the points of convergence are these:

1. *Atonement is an act of God.* At various places in the
New Testament, the Jews are given responsibility for the
crucifixion, or Jesus is described as offering himself for death,
yet finally it is clear that the act ultimately was of God. "God

was in Christ reconciling the world to himself" (2 Cor. 5:19). Even though secondary agents may be mentioned, finally it was God's act. The atonement proceeds directly out of God's love for his people. The giving of his Son is his gift—his gift so rich as to be unsearchable—for man's salvation. The New Testament declares that men are justified by God's grace "as a gift" and that the atonement is an aspect of God's love for men. The motive of love is emphasized strongly in the Johannine writings, but it is also present in Paul.

2. *Christ's death and resurrection are at the very center of the doctrine of the atonement.* The weight of New Testament evidence is that atonement is made primarily through Christ's death and resurrection, characteristically mentioned together.

Christ's climactic work is vicarious, representative, and sacrificial in nature. As vicarious, it is chiefly to be understood "on behalf of" mankind, rather than in man's place. Except for one statement (recorded in Mark 10:45 and Matt. 20:28), the preposition used in connection with Christ's death is *huper,* "on behalf of," and not *anti,* "instead of." *Huper* is so generally used as to suggest very strongly that the understanding of "vicarious" as "substitutionary" is a misplaced emphasis; Christ died "for our sake" rather than "in our place." The stress is thus on man's reconciliation to God, not God's to man. As Paul exulted in the Galatian letter (Gal. 2:20b), "I live by faith in the Son of God, who loved me and gave himself for [*huper*] me."

As representative, Christ's work is to be understood as that of the Suffering Servant, the reconciler or mediator, the sealer of the new covenant, who represents man and thereby enables man to come before God. Christ identified himself with men—here is the basis of his representative nature. As our representative, he makes it possible for us progressively to enter into the meaning and results of the atonement.

As sacrificial—and the repeated New Testament references to sacrificial imagery do not allow us to overlook this—Christ's work provides an objective means of entering into a saving relationship with God. For whatever reasons—dramatization of the terribleness of sin, maintenance of the moral balance of the world, necessary expiation for great wrongs—forgiveness involves sacrificial work, which Christ has provided. It was only as Christ took on the sacrificial work of atonement that men could come to know God.

The resurrection dramatizes the victory of Christ. The experience of the disciples convinced them that something of the highest significance had happened. It was then clear to them that God had sent his Son to be the one through whom the reconciliation would be accomplished, and that it was his life, death, and resurrection that was the crowning climax of the whole redemptive process. Resurrection and atonement are intimately related in Christian thinking; in Paul's words, "If Christ has not been raised, your faith is futile and you are still in your sins" (1 Cor. 15:17).

3. This leads into the next point, that *the work of atonement is directed toward removing the barrier of sin.* From the earliest statements in the eucharistic sayings and the apostolic preaching down to the Revelation to John, every New Testament writer connects the death of Christ with the forgiveness of sins. The particular understanding of the nature of sin and the explanation of the manner in which it is removed as a barrier between God and man differs, but the central problem is that of sin. Human sin necessitates an atonement; Christ's work is that effective means for the blotting out of sins. Men are caught in bondage to sin; Christ broke the power of sin over man. He sets us free, and enables us to accept God's love for us, the love which he revealed to us. He is not only Revealer, but Savior too. In Christ men see accomplished that which most needs to be

effected. It is too lofty for them to do themselves, but his act gives them opportunity for participation in divine realities and for appropriation of divine mercies through faith. There is, even after all the biblical themes have been studied and all the patterns of history bearing on the atonement have been reviewed, an irreducible core of mystery, for at this point we draw near to the heart of God, near to the immeasurable dimension of his love and the unimaginable glory of his grace.

4. *Men participate in the atonement by repentance and faith.* Here the truth of the subjective pattern is evident. For, although Christ's obedience and suffering were his own, they were on our behalf and therefore generally of benefit to all men and indeed to all creation. But we can appropriate their benefits only as we repent of our sins and throw ourselves on the mercy of God in faith. Through our faith-union with Christ, through communion with him and through sacrificial living and suffering, the atonement made by Christ on our behalf is received and appropriated by us.

This appropriation, however, is by faith. Atonement and justification are two sides of the same act of God, one dealing with what God has done in Christ and the other with man's appropriation of its benefits, made possible by the gift of faith. The doctrine of justification by faith is perhaps the key religious problem for modern man as he struggles to understand and grasp historic Christian faith. Here the Christian doctrines of God and man are joined.

Justification by grace through faith is a description of what happens in the encounter between divinity and the believing man. It is not abstract speculation but the very dynamic of the Christian life. It roots in what may be called "a biblical view of life." This view begins with the unquestioned fact of the holy sovereign God, whose ways are not our ways, whose face is hid from us, yet who confronts us men—first corporately, then individually. Finally no one can escape God, because all are creatures of his making. The only question is one of relationship. The Old Testament theme of the covenant relationship between the Israelite community and the LORD GOD is the story of that struggle to relate. In the New Testament, with the close-knit national covenant replaced in one sense and yet fulfilled through the revelation in Christ, the new relationship is identified as justification by grace through faith. This is in many ways a restoration of what had been the foundation of the old covenant in ancient Israel—namely, the utter dependability of God's initiative, the completeness of what God provides for human life. But under the old covenant, men failed to live according to what had been given to them. In the fullness of time, God showed his concern for the world in the life, death, and resurrection of Christ.

The New Testament unfolds this act of God not in speculative terms but in the recounting of the event, in the presentation of the facts which faith understands to be revelatory. Faith acknowledges our complete insufficiency for any of the high ends of life, and finds that we must rely utterly on the sufficiency of God, whose limitless love is vividly dramatized by incarnation and atonement. Where men failed to live under the initial covenant, their justification is now, under the new covenant, wholly the consequence of God's grace, received through faith.

All this cuts across the conceptions which modern man often has of the encounter between himself and God. He is prone to begin with himself, to believe that the solutions to all questions insofar as they may be obtained lie within reach of an exploration of his own experiences and aspirations. He is inclined to believe that disciplined and rigorous search will lead him to God, make plain his nature, and justify the ways of God to man.

It is precisely here that contemporary psychiatric understanding can be a tremendous asset to the clarification of the doctrine of justification by faith. For it is today well understood that fearless exploration of the recesses of one's own life may be essential to health, that the measure of one's own guilt must be faced and accepted. Such an acknowledgment must of necessity begin personally; with Isaiah of old we cry, "Woe is me! for I am undone; because I am a man of unclean lips." But the process of confession of sin moves outwards: "I dwell in the midst of a people of unclean lips." It moves outwards until it becomes a statement about the whole human situation: "all have sinned and fall short of the glory of God."

It seems nearly impossible for God's independent initiating action to be experienced or understood until the futility of man's attempt to save himself is plainly experienced. It is only when man has exhausted and emptied himself of false ideologies, both personal and cultural, that the God and Father of our Lord Jesus Christ truly becomes "my God," and I know that my justification is only by grace and through faith—only then does God become "our God, our help in ages past, our hope for years to come."

The chasm between sinful man and the Almighty and Eternal God, infinite in holiness, pure in justice and love, is bridged by the cross of Christ. Here God dissolves the distinctions of justice and mercy as far as his acceptance of man is concerned; here by faith alone we who are sinful are made righteous. The full significance of the incarnation becomes clear in the cross. For incarnation does not mean simply that God sent his Son into his creation in human form. It means God the Son was obedient unto death, that he accepted the final sacrilege, the suffering of death at the hands of God's own creatures, to show forth the magnitude of the Father's love. He faced the full despair of death to remove its sting for them that believe. When in faith we confess that of ourselves we can do nothing, but can only throw ourselves on the mercy of God in loving trust, then we are justified; then not we alone, but Christ also liveth in us.

BIBLIOGRAPHY

Aulen, Gustav E., *Christus Victor*. New York: The Macmillan Company, 1934, 179 pp.

Baillie, Donald M., *God Was in Christ*. New York: Charles Scribner's Sons, 1948, 213 pp.

Franks, Robert S., *The Atonement*. London: Oxford University Press, 1934, 202 pp.

Mathews, Shailer, *The Atonement and the Social Process*. New York: The Macmillan Company, 1930, 212 pp.

Miller, Alexander, *The Renewal of Man: A Twentieth Century Essay on Justification by Faith*. Garden City, New York: Doubleday and Company, 1955, 184 pp.

Rashdall, Hastings, *The Idea of the Atonement in Christian Theology*. London: The Macmillan Company, Ltd., 1920, 502 pp.

Robinson, Henry Wheeler, *Redemption and Revelation in the Actuality of History*. New York: Harper & Brothers, 1942, 320 pp.

Taylor, Vincent, *The Atonement in New Testament Teaching*. 2nd ed.; London: The Epworth Press, 1950, 221 pp.

————, *Forgiveness and Reconciliation: A Study in New Testament Theology*. 2nd ed.; London: The Macmillan Company, 1946, 242 pp.

Wolf, William J., *No Cross No Crown*. Garden City, New York: Doubleday and Company, 1957, 216 pp.

VI

A BAPTIST THEOLOGY OF CHURCH ORDER

HARRY H. KRUENER

I. THE MEANING OF CHURCH ORDER

IT IS NECESSARY in a treatise of this kind to state rather specifically what we mean when we use terms which are unfamiliar or have fallen into misuse. Our Baptist people have not always been sure that "church order" has anything to do with our Baptist witness which traditionally seems to have been one of freedom and spontaneity in the life of the churches. However, I think if we look closely at the word and its meaning it will become clear that the whole church has had something to do with "church order" from its very beginning.

Paul, in the 14th chapter of 1 Corinthians, talks about the confusion and disorderliness of the church when it came together for worship. His final plea is to let all things in the church be "done decently and in order." Many of the Epistles were written to problems of church order. From the New Testament times down to the present, the problem of "order"

149

has been one for all the branches of Christendom. It is the shape which the church takes confronting the world. This shape depends on the understanding of the mission of the church or the works the church must do in the world. In our Baptist tradition, though it is one of freedom and spontaneity, there is also concern for discipline and church government duly executed. There are certain works of the church, such as: the faithful proclamation of the Word of God, the regular administration of the ordinances of baptism and the Lord's Supper, a ministry sufficiently gifted and learned so as to lead the congregation, and a congregational organization which oversees the ministries of worship, evangelism, education, mutual care, and service.

It is perhaps needless to say that the primary contribution of Baptists has not been in this province of church order and its theological understanding, but it is certain that the Baptist protest against a rigid, inflexible, and static church order has been an important one. This protest recognizes that the "order" of a church, its rites and polity, is clearly in the realm of the historically contingent. To insist that a particular "church order," unchanged and sanctified from the beginning, is the only possible one is a form of sinful spiritual imperialism.

We must realize, however, that though this church order, this shape of the church in the world, must be of such a nature as to speak to the historical situation in which it finds itself, it does not follow that church order is mere cultural expediency. That "order" must be founded on the spirit of Jesus Christ as it speaks to the church in every age. The church must never merely conform to the world. Church order must be relevant to history but not determined by it.

To define specifically, Baptists are spoken of as having "free" church order, of being "congregational" in polity, "democratic" in government, or as having "local autonomy."

All of these terms attempt to describe the same thing, namely, the structure of the local Baptist church, its relationships with other Baptist churches, and with other churches of Christ and the Ecumenical Movement.

The task of this paper will be not so much to describe the practice of Baptist churches in this regard as to inquire into the fundamental thinking or theology behind this structure and practice. In theological circles Baptists are known as believers in "the gathered church." The term comes from the word of our Lord in Matt. 18:20: "For where two or three are gathered in my name, there am I in the midst of them." The church is a fellowship gathered in Christ's name. This stands in distinction from, first of all, the horizontal theories of the church, which stresses its hierarchy and history. For such, the true church has a common authority, a duly-ordained apostolically-sanctioned ministry, and a uniformity of organization. It stands, also, in distinction from the vertical theories of the church, which stress that the church is where the Word is preached and the Sacraments administered. Baptists and others of congregational organization claim that there is a third definition of the church which stresses the fellowship of the Spirit, a characteristic not sufficiently recognized in the other two. The task of this paper, then, will be to analyze what we mean theologically by a "gathered church," starting with the New Testament. We will attempt to see what this implies for the individual church member, the local church in its ministry and business meetings, the association of churches and, finally, the relationship of Baptists to other bodies of Christians. We will not so much describe how Baptist churches work as how they think. What are the theological presuppositions, consciously or unconsciously implicit, behind a church order that we like to call "free"?

II. THE "GATHERED CHURCH" IN THE NEW TESTAMENT

In the opening sentences to his paper on "The Nature of the Church," John Skoglund writes: "Baptists never have gone into too much detail about the nature of the church. They have been content to say that theirs is a New Testament church." [1] What may be said generally about the nature of the church certainly can be said about more specific areas. In matters such as church order, organization, discipline, polity, ministry, Baptists have just presumed that theirs is the New Testament pattern and they have faithfully sought to work accordingly. To say whether this presumption is justified or not is our first task. As Baptists we must spell out in greater detail what we mean by a New Testament church.

It should be said right off that the New Testament church does not present itself as any one fixed organization, or one form of worship, or one type of ministry, which we can then proceed without any difficulty to imitate. Many Christian communions can conscientiously claim to derive their polity and church order from the New Testament. Baptists are aware that "bishops" and "presbyters" and "priests" and "elders" are mentioned as well as "deacons" and "ministers." However, in studying the total picture of the early church, Baptists have been convinced that the basic unit of the New Testament church is the "gathered church." It is the "congregation gathered by God through Christ."

The church in the New Testament is not an institution as such, but a people, God's people. This is not to deny that institutions have their rightful and necessary place, but the church is greater than any institution and must always re-

---

[1] John Skoglund, "The Nature of the Church," a paper presented before the Theological Conference, Green Lake, 1954.

main so. Nor can its essential nature be found in any person or ecclesiastical authority. The true New Testament church is a congregation of the faithful. In 1611, Thomas Helwys in "A Declaration of Faith of English People Remaining in Holland" wrote: "We believe and confess . . . that the church of Christ is a company of faithful people separated from the world by the Word and Spirit of God, being knit into the Lord and unto one another, by baptism upon their own confession of the faith." In our own times the Baptist Union of Great Britain replied to the Lambeth Appeal with the words: "We believe in the Catholic Church as the holy society of believers in our Lord Jesus Christ, which He founded, of which He is the only Head, and in which He dwells by His Spirit." For Baptists, then, it is clear that the New Testament church is not an institution but a people, a society, a company, a congregation gathered by God through Christ.

This concept of the church as a people, God's people, derives from the Old Testament's central theme of God's covenant with Israel. This covenant started with Abraham and is imprinted on the consciousness of Israel in the Exodus and the giving of the Law. The Christian church inherits the covenant when the Jews fail, when they make the Law a barrier rather than a road to God, transforming the covenant into a contract seeking to have God on their own terms. The church is the "true Israel of God."

It is small wonder then that in the early days of Christianity synagogue and *ecclēsia* (the New Testament word for church) are used interchangeably. They both refer to an assembly, a congregation, meeting for any purpose, civic or religious. They are both derived in their languages from a root-verb meaning "to gather." In the Book of James (cf. James 2:2, KJV) "synagogue" is used to denote an assembly of Christians and in the Book of Hebrews (cf. Heb. 10:25, KJV) Christians are exhorted not to forsake "the assembling [synagoguing] of ourselves together." With the death of Stephen and the increasing split between Christianity and Judaism, *ecclēsia* emerges as the distinctly Christian term and synagogue the Jewish. We cannot fail to note, however, that the very language of Judaism is carried over into the early days of Christianity. The "gathered church" is really a continuation of "the gathered synagogue of Israel." In both, the authority is in the congregation.

Jesus himself never specifically founded an organization called the church. He spoke of the church only twice (cf. Matt. 16:18; 18:17). His message was about the Kingdom. Some scholars have concluded, therefore, that the church was entirely a creation of our Lord's apostles, something that never occurred to him. This, on second thought, proves to be a hasty conclusion. For if our Lord never organized a church, the church idea was certainly in his mind from the start. He certainly "gathered" a congregation about himself. He sent his disciples forth to preach "in his name." His disciples might have been gathered informally but they were never gathered casually. The Twelve represent the twelve tribes of "the new Israel." His teaching is directed not so much to individuals as to a community of believers. His acceptance of the messianic title or that of Son of man implies in itself the creation of a new community. Indeed, his constant controversies with the Pharisees and Sadducees must be seen as much more than a clash between religious individualism and institutionalism or a struggle between a creative personality and the vested interests; actually Jesus' entire ministry may have been directed toward making clear to his opponents the nature and membership of "the new Covenant, the true Israel" as distinct from the old and dying. If Jesus never organized a church, he certainly consciously gathered a community about himself. He said: "Where two or three are gathered in my name, there am I in the midst." The early church believed that when it assembled it assembled both in the name and intent of its Lord.

This "true Israel" was brought into being by Christ's death and resurrection. The descent of the Spirit and the founding of the church are bound up intimately with the work of Christ in his life, death, and rising again. The church is actually the community that responds to the resurrection. It is in this sense "the extension of the incarnation," as Anglican theology often defines it. Pentecost was both an individual and a corporate experience of the Risen Christ. Individually they knew him for "tongues of fire sat on the head of each of them present;" but as a community they also knew him for the Holy Spirit was as a "rushing mighty wind that filled the house."

Paul seeks to describe this church. The church is a "building," or a "temple" in which God dwells, of which Christ is the chief cornerstone holding the walls together and saving the building from collapse. Or the church is "the body of Christ" of which we are members. Christ is the head of the body. Christ is sovereign and the church is subject unto Christ (cf. Eph. 5:22-23). All these figures stress the corporate nature of the church, its organic unity. All of them stress the lordship of Christ. Paul's doctrine of the church is derived from his doctrine of Christ. From this biblical background we can arrive at some conclusions about the New Testament church.

1. The New Testament church is not an institution but a people, God's people. It is not an organization gathered about an apostle or church ecclesiastic. It is a "congregation gathered by God through Christ," a continuance of the congregation of Israel.

2. The New Testament church knows nothing of what we would call rugged individualism. The early Christians had a great sense of the community into which every Chris-

tian was brought by the Spirit. Solitary religion was unthinkable. Just as God in the past made his covenant with a group, the nation of Israel, so God made his new covenant in Christ with another group, the church, the true Israel. No individual is saved apart from the Christian community. He cannot live apart from "the body." The church is not a convenience placed at the disposal of the individual; it is an indispensable spiritual necessity.

3. The New Testament church has its unity in Christ. Again, it is no human contrivance to get ahead in the world or be better organized or more efficient. The church is "gathered by God through Christ." "Where Christ is there is the Church," the earliest church fathers said. We are gathered "in His Name." His Lordship can be seen in the past, in that the church is the community that responded to his life, death, and resurrection; hence Paul speaks of baptism as baptism into his death and resurrection (cf. Rom. 6:4). He is head of the church in the present, and in the future he shall be "all in all."

4. The New Testament church is holy. Holy refers to "wholeness." This wholeness of the church is known only to God and the church as we know it is obviously not whole. We all therefore have a dual citizenship and the earthly church is at best a "colony of heaven." Moreover, the parable of the wheat and the tares warns us against the inevitable intermingling of good and evil until harvest. However, we must be careful in the light of the New Testament not to fall into an easy dualism between the Church Visible and the Church Invisible, whereby we look upon the earthly church as only a poor and imperfect copy of some heavenly ideal above. This dualism is more akin to Platonic philosophy which separates the Ideal from the Real than to the New Testament, and such a dualism can easily lead to a feeling of irresponsibility toward the earthly church. With all its flaws,

the church here and now partakes of the wholeness, the holiness, of the Church. The New Testament makes no facile separation between real and ideal.

5. The New Testament church is apostolic. However, we must notice that it is the faith of the apostles, their witness to Christ, that constitutes their authority rather than their persons. The value of "apostolic succession" is to emphasize the historical continuity, the horizontal continuity in time, between Christ and the believer. The church is not only vertical in its relationship to Christ, but horizontal: Christ with his apostles and with his church. The New Testament does not separate, as some liberal scholars have, the Jesus of history from the Christ of faith or the Christ the head of the church. This led to the "quest of the historical Jesus," a quest now proved hopeless, with its "modernizing" of Jesus into a figure human, poetic, romantic, and distinctly un-theological. We might as well accept the continuity of faith from Jesus through the apostles through the early church. In this sense, on the authority of the faith and witness of the apostles, the New Testament church is apostolic.

6. The New Testament church is catholic and universal. This does not mean that there was uniformity of organization or any single allegiance to bishop, presbyter, apostle, or elder. The congregation, synagogue, or *ecclēsia,* always had three meanings; one, the universal—the congregation of Israel in toto; the second, the local—referring to the local group gathered in a specific town or building; third, the universal mission of Israel or the church to gather all into its fellowship, so that the *ecclēsia* was never just an exclusive group keeping the covenant to itself. Hence catholicity is never diametrically opposed to local church gatherings. In the New Testament there were many local congregations formed, varied in structure and leadership, but these local congregations never thought of themselves as autonomous,

or totally independent of each other. The very word for church is an organic word uniting both the local and the universal. All local churches in the New Testament had a real sense of the Church Universal and of its mission. In turn, we may also notice that the Church Universal manifested itself in gathered local companies of believers without any sense of conflict or loss of universality. Congregationalism, except where it seeks complete local autonomy, is not the opposite of catholicity. In the New Testament the two go hand in hand.

7. Finally, the New Testament church is a church in pilgrimage toward that day when Christ will return to claim his bride. In this eschatological sense, rather than in any Platonic philosophical sense, the church is "invisible." Its wholeness is yet to be realized at the end of history.

III. THE "GATHERED CHURCH" IN BAPTIST PRACTICE

So much for the New Testament background of "the gathered church," "the congregation gathered by God through Christ." But now we must ask: How true have Baptists been to their New Testament heritage? What has been their practice? Has it always fitted into the New Testament pattern described above? Where not, what theologies, or philosophies, or ideas, other than the New Testament, have crept in? What should we re-emphasize today to restore our Baptist thinking to its New Testament heritage? What should belief in the congregation as the basic unit of the church mean today?

Needless to say, this paper cannot go into any detailed analysis of the history of the Baptists and their changing theology of church order during the last four centuries. All we can hope to do is to point out in the contemporary scene some attitudes, statements of belief and practice, some widely-held points of view, which must be examined in the light of the New Testament. We shall do this in five areas.

Area One: The Meaning of Individualism in Church Life

One Baptist distinctive is called the doctrine of soul-competency. If this means the individual believer standing alone before God, it is a distortion of the Christian experience as described in the New Testament. There is no such thing as solitary religion. Conversion, the experience of being saved, is never isolated from the Christian community, and the converted believer never continues in isolation; he joins the church. The church, therefore, is not an option, it is a necessity for the believer. It can never be defined as merely the sum total of saved individuals who may or may not wish to assemble together. Such attitudes as "I can be a perfectly good Christian without ever participating in the church," or "A good Baptist church is made up of rugged individuals where every man has his own religion and one man's opinion is as good as another," or "God speaks to me directly and I don't need a group, because religion is a "flight of the alone with the alone," or "I belong to the Church Invisible; why should I bother with the imperfect and hypocritical visible church?"— these represent trends in 18th and 19th century American democracy, based upon the philosophy of the Enlightenment and reflecting the individualism of the frontier rather than the New Testament.

The doctrine of soul-competency can be seen most clearly in the statements of two able Baptist scholars, H. Wheeler Robinson of England and William Roy McNutt, for many years professor at Crozer Seminary, whose book *Polity and Practice in Baptist Churches* has long been a standard for the interpretation of our church order. H. Wheeler Robinson speaks of all true religion as a "personal thing" and the churches as only "associations of religious men." [2] Dr. McNutt writes:

> The individual is competent in all matters of religion; he has within himself by divine gift the capacities for religion. . . . He has no inescapable need of the church to bring him salvation or mediate to him divine grace. . . . It is the doctrine of soul-competency that produces the Baptist doctrine of the church.[3]

This doctrine, Professor McNutt believes, exalts the common man, and by virtue of this divinely-bestowed competency it follows that all men are free. It is an inalienable right. He goes on to stay that all authority is within the individual. "Baptist doctrine sets each man on a throne." We may counsel with others, call them to our throne, but each man alone is responsible. He concludes that the purpose of this doctrine of soul-competency is to produce the individual Christian, "tall, straight, and clean as a southern pine."

We should notice immediately the absence of quotations from the New Testament to defend this thesis and the reiteration of phrases which are common in the secular literature of the Enlightenment and its interpretations of democracy. "Inalienable right, the common man, freedom by divine right, each man a king, the rugged individual standing alone against the sky like a pine"—these have a familiar ring. They are dear to the heritage of the Revolution and the frontier of America. Soul-competency sounds like another "declaration of independence" from all authority, spiritual or secular. The picture is of the solitary individual, who may now and again assemble with others, consult with them, but feels no need of such a group experience. Basically he keeps his own

---

[2] From *The Life and Faith of the Baptists*, by H. Wheeler Robinson; Methuen & Co. Ltd., London, 1927.

[3] From *Polity and Practice in Baptist Churches*, pp. 21 ff., by William Roy McNutt; copyright, 1935, The Judson Press, Philadelphia.

counsel in all matters spiritual. He feels completely competent by himself to interpret Scripture, by himself to be converted, by himself to worship God, and by himself and in the light of his own conscience, to stand before God's throne of Judgment.

For such a rugged individualist the church is an option. Individualism leads to voluntarism: he may or may not join a church, it is entirely voluntary. The job of the church is really to convert individuals, then go out and organize them, then get them to apply for membership in some Baptist association. Notice, the church is never part of the conversion experience itself, either before or after. The believer stands alone before God. The church at its best is a clearing-house for converts, a convenience, whose highest test is its organizational efficiency. At its worst it is a hindrance to the spiritual life. So far as the visible church goes, this sort of Baptist is an idealist. He can take it or leave it. He knows himself to be part of the Church Invisible and is satisfied. Church order for him is merely a convenience, a "human contrivance."

Many a Baptist believes this to be the essence of the Baptist faith, and our churches are full of such rugged individualists for whom the church is a casual convenience, or else an arena where the ego can strut like a Daniel Boone or a Davey Crockett. It is enough to point out that such a person, and such a doctrine of soul-competency, reflects the Enlightenment more than the New Testament.

This individualism of our Baptist churches has not developed in a vacuum.[4] One of the greatest influences was the 17th century English philosopher, John Locke. It is no accident that Locke's dates, spreading across the middle and late years of the 17th century correspond almost exactly with

---

[4] The research for this section of the paper was done by my colleague in the Theological Conference, the Rev. Howard Moody of Judson Baptist Church, New York City.

the years in which the pattern of free church polity was in formation. The whole 17th century saw a decisive turn from the political tradition stemming from Plato, Aristotle, and the Middle Ages of man as citizen, to a new individualistic contract theory of society. Until the 17th century man as member of community served as the basic axiom and man the individual was the derivative. But to the 17th century social thinkers, casting about for a theoretical basis for the political changes they were witnessing, the individual man seemed to be the surest, most "self-evident" starting point. Relations always appeared thinner than substances to these alert political theorists. Man was the substance; society was the relation. Obviously the individual was both logically and ethically prior.

This insistence on the basic character of the inherent rights of the individual is understandable in an age when individual rights were being more and more insisted upon. John Locke's keystone, man's inherent right to life, liberty, and property, became the source of Jefferson's "inalienable rights"—with pursuit of happiness substituted for property. For Locke, as for the founders of American society, the main function of governments and of society itself was to insure these rights. Society exists, that is, to protect private property and other rights which society does not create. The power of the community, for Locke, is no more than the natural power of each man resigned "into the hands of the community" (*Of Civil Government,* Book II, section 99) and justified simply because it is a better way of protecting natural rights than the self-help to which each man is entitled.

This has produced the voluntaristic view of the church, so influential in Baptist circles. But can this now be accepted as valid New Testament truth about the church? "Individual Christianity," whether of believer or congregation, is, as Aulen says, a *"contradictio in adjecto."* Christian life and faith is both born and nurtured in the fellowship of the church. Jesus constantly asserts that preparation for the new age of the Reign of God involves entry into the new community which comes into being with the preaching of the gospel. The church, the "new people among the people," is an integral part of God's work of redemption. Individualism, if it is taken to mean isolation of the individual, is in fact just that sinful condition *from* which man is delivered in and through faith.

According to the New Testament, God redeems men by bringing them into the new community of faith and wholeness. The church thus belongs to Jesus Christ. It is not constituted by individuals with certain definite religious qualifications. It is not the end result of a contract by like-minded individuals, but is the fellowship of the Holy Spirit, the sphere of Chirst's dominion. A Christian, then, may be "saved" by an act of choice of Jesus Christ, and in this act of freedom the soul is truly "competent" before God and men. But he does not come as a solitary individual to this choice and never will.

Nor does the Christian go forth from the experience of salvation to walk alone before God. He is saved to become a member of Christ's body, the divine society, the church. The essence of salvation is repentence, faith in Christ, and obedience to Christ. The New Testament cannot conceive of such salvation coming in solitary fashion or producing rugged individualism. "Do you despise the church of God?" cries Paul (1 Cor. 11:22). It seemed incredible to him that any believer could do so.

Baptists must, therefore, be careful that their interpretation of conversion, of salvation, is complete, not partial. Conversion is not a highly charged, emotional urge, devoid of any sense of the Christian community, and issuing in a fastidious idealism or disdain of the visible church and its responsibilities. This is the "misunderstanding of the church" which Emil Brunner finds so insidious in Christian history. In this "misunderstanding" the "Invisible Church" was made up of elect individuals and the "Visible Church" was then purely an earthly institution. This dualism is unknown to the New Testament. The New Testament knows nothing of such other worldliness; it is too history-conscious. So, the Baptist today must realize the corporate nature of his own conversion-experience, and he must go forth to live responsibly in that community of faith which is the church visible and on earth. The church for him then becomes not a disjointed group of individuals organized for human efficiency; it is an organism, a body of which Christ is the Head and each of us members one of another. To know Christ is to recognize your part in his body and to find that your competency, far from being in your own soul, is in the congregation, the community of faith and work, which he has gathered unto himself.

Strangely enough, this is in line with most modern psychology. Modern social psychologists and depth psychologists have long since undercut the social contract theory of society and human relationships. The discreet individual who then freely enters into relationships in society never existed except in the minds of social contract theorists. Man becomes an individual only within a matrix of relationships. Without these he never becomes a person. His selfhood is the emergent result of his relationships from childhood on. Both theologians and psychologists are beginning to see relatedness as the very nature and basis of human selfhood.

We need only add a practical note, that in our membership classes and in the receiving of members into our Baptist churches this "higher" theology of the church should be stressed. Any doctrine of soul-competency must be secondary to the New Testament doctrine of the church, not primary as Dr. McNutt suggests. Members must realize that the church is more than a club, joined by individuals who happen to prefer it to other clubs. It is more than a human contrivance. It is the community of faith from which our individual faith never stands apart. Members thus theologically-grounded will be both more humble and more responsible to the body of Christ.

Area Two: The Laity and the Ministry

For Baptists the ministry of a local church is a "mutual ministry of all believers." It relies as much on the laity as on the pastor; indeed, we may assert the primacy of the laity, believing that Baptists not only carry the Reformation principle of "the priesthood of all believers" to its logical conclusion, but also that they follow the New Testament references in Paul and in 1 Pet. 2 where he speaks of a "royal priesthood." The distinction is never between clergy and laity as such, but only between "spiritual gifts." It is never an intrinsic; it is a functional distinction.

This radical concept of the primacy of the laity not only indicates that there can be no inherent religious difference between the laity and the ministry, it also means that the major responsibility for the proper maintenance of the church is given to the whole congregation. The full implications of this will be discussed later in a section on the congregational meeting. However, this means that it is incumbent upon the whole community of believers to see that the witness of the church is in accord with the Word of God. However, it is hardly necessary to point out that in those church traditions which proclaim this truth most vividly, the churches have become "pastor-centered" and the congregation does not assume its full responsibility.

We must raise the question: What is the nature of the ministry in our churches, given this minimizing of the difference between the laity and the ministry? In the free-church conception of the ministry it is a ministry of a church and not a ministry of an individual. It is the church which preaches the Word and administers the ordinances. It normally does these things through its minister, but not solely through him. The minister is called out by the congregation to be their pastor. He derives his authority from Christ through the congregation of God's people. The ministry belongs to the congregation. But not only is the minister the servant of his people, he is "minister verbi divini," "the servant of the Word of God." It is in his keeping to bring, through his special call, gifts, and training, the Word of God to his people. There is some sense in which the minister is not only the servant of the people of his congregation but responsible to God to help the local congregation see itself and its vocation in the setting of the whole purpose of God for all his people.

Also, as pertains to the order of the church, the minister is not only the minister of a local congregation, but he is a representative of the whole church of God to the local community of believers. Daniel Jenkins in his little book *Congregationalism; A Restatement* puts it this way:

> When a local church gathers around the Bible on the Lord's Day to hear what God is speaking to it from His Word, it will lose touch with the Spirit of God and mishear His Word if it steps out of the context of this rich experience (i.e., of the universal Church through all ages) which is, of course, not only the experience of the Bible itself, but what God has said and done to His people through all history and what He is doing now in His dealings with them. It is the purpose of the minister to do this on behalf of the Church.[5]

───────────

[5] From *Congregationalism: A Restatement,* by Daniel Jenkins; copyright 1954, Harper and Brothers, New York.

In the Baptist statement at the Conference on Faith and Order at Lund, Sweden, one section says:

> Since the ministry is the gift of God to the Church and the call to exercise the function of the ministry comes from Him, a man who is so called is not only the minister of a local Baptist church, but also a minister of the whole Church of Jesus Christ.

This means that insofar as the minister is the true representative of the Universal Church to the local church, the order of the church is determined not solely by the local fellowship of believers, but in part by the whole history of God's dealing with his people in the church.

It is not meant by this inference that there is any particularly holy and inflexible order handed down from Christ himself to the apostles for the ordering of the church, or that the minister has authority by virtue of his connection with some "apostolic succession." For Baptists, at least, the essence of true apostleship was not to be identified with ordination into a select circle or lineage, but rather in the faithful witness to the truth of the Christian gospel as revealed by the Holy Spirit.

To sum up, the ministry and the laity each plays a unique and significant role in that "mutual ministry of all believers" which ultimately is responsible for ordering and sustaining the life of a local congregation of believers.

Area Three: The Nature of the Church Meeting

Flowing out of the important doctrine of the "mutual ministry of all believers" is emphasis on the church meeting. Baptists have always prided themselves on the democratic form of their church polity, in the fact that the decisions about church order and life did not rest solely with the ministry, but were made by the people of the congregation, thus avoiding clericalism and ecclesiastical domination. However, though in theory the congregational meeting was the answer we claimed to these threats, in our own Baptist churches, it has degenerated into an annual meeting at which reports are given. There is a sense in which we have denied a basic principle of our forefathers, namely, that we are members of one another and we must come together and share our understanding of the will of God, as made known to us through Jesus Christ, for the discipline and order of our common life.

No Christian thinker in modern times has perturbed our thinking and pointed up our weaknesses in this regard like Dr. Daniel Jenkins.[6] The place where the laity must take up its responsibility for the direction and ordering of the church's life is the church meeting. Dr. Jenkins finds this principle of congregationalism in the institution of the of the church meeting. I think we as Baptists may find this same principle embodied historically in the "covenant meetings" of our earlier Baptist churches.

It is in our keeping also to discover the theological bases upon which our congregational polity is validated. For example, we sometimes seem to justify our Baptist type of church government and order by the fact that it is "democratic," as if this were the ultimate justification. This is an inadequate theological test for the life of the church. If the church be the body of Christ and its Head is our Lord, the talk of democracy is not altogether appropriate. Christ's kingdom is a monarchy and not a democracy. We do not come together in the life of a church simply to express an opinion, or to vote on what we think is the way to do our task. We come together to hear the Word of God speak to our situation and the Spirit of Christ to be manifest so that our opinions and

---

[6] See the bibliography at the end of this chapter.

prejudices may be transformed into his holy will. If there be democracy in the church, it is not because one person's opinion is as good as the next, but because under Christ, every human person is a free and responsible being under God worthy of being heard.

The purpose of the meeting in the life of the local church is not to determine the will of the majority of members on certain institutional aspects of the church's life. The meeting is for the purpose of the members seeking each other's help to discern the will of God for a particular local congregation in the community which it finds itself. If our Baptist churches, rather than spending their time reading sheaves of mimeographed reports and deliberating on such weighty matters as whether the choir shall process or the furnace shall be lit Saturday night rather than Sunday morning, could really spend time in its meetings seeking the will of God for that church, what is its task and mission and how do the activities of that church contribute to the mission, then our meetings might come alive and God might perchance speak through them.

The meeting of the congregation must be a vital and significant part of the church's common life; it cannot be divorced from worship, communion, and prayer, as though the congregational meeting were simply that time when the secular or material aspects of the church's life were discussed and through the pooling of common sense and the majority will we somehow arrive at what the church ought to do. The church meeting ought to be imbued with the same high experience as worship, and we ought here to be able to partake of God's grace even as we do in the Lord's Supper. Given this concept of the spiritual significance of the meeting of the church—that is, a vehicle used by God to open to his people new truths and bring them through their common seeking to a new obedience—it is perhaps most desirable that the minister officiate and head the meeting even as he leads the congregation in the preaching of the Word and the administering of the ordinances. Once again the minister, not because of any authority which he possesses but only because of his call and gifts and learnedness, leads his people in this act of the common life. As has been pointed out, no court of law would think of convening without someone present learned in legal matters to preside, so the church ought not to meet without a minister, steeped in God's Word, cognizant of the church of Jesus Christ in all the world, to give his guidance and counsel to the people.

We Baptists have in our history and traditional polity the means to revive the life of our churches provided we can recover and articulate the theological bases upon which they rest. In this way alone we can save the churches from secularization. The local church is the microcosm of the Great Church. It is here that people find their lives, hear the Word preached, receive the sacraments, and strive to live out the life of Christ in the world. Only as this local church hears the word of Christ speak to it can it so order its life and ministries as to bring God's healing and redeeming love to people who so desperately need it. The encouraging hope of our Baptist churches is that because of our freedom and flexibility we can change our polity in the interests of spiritual power for ministering to the world.

Area Four: The Association and the Convention

Baptists understand the word "church" to refer to the whole or universal company of believers AND to the local congregation.[7] Associations, state and national, are therefore not secondary or tertiary relationships into which local

---

[7] The research for this section of the paper was done by my colleague in the Theological Conference, the Rev. Harvey Cox, of the Y.M.C.A., Oberlin College, Ohio.

churches may or may not enter, but are in fact expressions of the very life of the church in its unity and universality. Any separatist interpretation of the autonomy of the local church is a theological error.

To understand local autonomy we must return again to John Locke and his concept of the individual isolated from the community. This individualistic principle was applied by Baptists not only to the relation of the individual belonging to the local congregation, but also to the relation of the local congregation to the fellowship of the denomination. It is dignified with the name "the autonomy of the local church."

This principle decisively influenced the polity of the early English Independents—Quakers, Baptists, and Congregationalists. We can understand why. It was just what they needed to escape the burdensome and authoritarian pressure of the religious hierarchy at the moment. But is was never accepted with the uncritical completeness with which it was swept into the American free churches. The early English Baptists, for instance, did not conceive of it in terms of congregational *autonomy,* which to later churches in America came to mean an isolation from the rest of the church, the nonbiblical notion that individual congregations could or could not enter into fellowship with others as they chose. Nor did the early English Baptists ever lose sight of the priority of the fellowship of the redeemed in the life of the individual believer. The concept of the church as a voluntaristic association of believers, constituted by a sort of social contract among them, never received wide acceptance.

It remained for the American churches to absolutize this autonomy of the local congregation. This was done in the name of "freedom" and even the New Testament. Needless to say, as we have pointed out above, the New Testament knows nothing of either the isolated Christian or the isolated Baptist congregation. A local congregation *is* an organic part

of every other congregation. It can deny this by being independent, but in doing so it shuts off its own source of life
and nourishment. It is a branch separated from the vine.

Since complete local autonomy cannot be maintained, in
lieu of the New Testament, what can we say about the
organization of Baptist churches into associations and conven-
tions from a theological point of view? We would like to
discuss two very practical questions in this area: 1. The
nature of the ministry of the executive secretary of the convention; and 2. The theological basis for any change in our
convention structure. For instance, was a report by the American Institute of Management, under discussion in our American Baptist Convention, a proper basis for a change of our
denominational polity?

First, then, consider the ministry of the executive secretary.
In the Baptist denomination, the executive secretary is clearly
a minister of the church. He serves a larger and more geo-
graphically scattered flock than a local minister, but minister he is. This vocation has several facets.

First of all, he is not there *simply* to carry out the wishes
of his constituency. This conception of a calling is just as
unthinkable in the ministry of the executive secretary as it in
the local parish. He is called to *lead,* to exhort, to criticize,
to teach, to minister. His loyalty is first to Christ the Lord of
the church and then to the denominational policies which
he is called upon to implement. The executive secretary's
leadership might be examined under the traditional head-
ings of the marks of the church, for in the deepest sense maintaining *the* church and *a* church is his basic assignment.

The traditional marks of the church: holiness, oneness,
apostolicity, and catholicity are affirmed by Baptists. We feel
that we are especially committed to the church's holiness,
hence regenerate church membership, and to its apostolicity,
hence our insistence upon the genuine biblical and apostolic

kerygma. If it is true that Baptists have not been as interested as they might be in the church's oneness and universality, an increased emphasis on these should in no way diminish our loyalty to its holiness and its apostolicity.

The church's holiness is an expression of the ethical and moral purity of its life, a purity which is God's gift and not its own creation. Churches betray this holiness in different ways in different times. "Worldliness," that is, reflecting the standards and evaluations of the "world" can easily become confused with moralism, even so-called "petty moralism." However, a church's practice with regard to racial inclusion, class divisions, materialistic standards of success and status achievement may be far more indicative of its degree of "worldliness" than the piety and moral practices of its individual members, as important as these are. An executive secretary who does not bring to bear the exhortation and concern of the whole church and of the gospel on churches whose life is exhibiting such "worldliness" is not accepting the full responsibilities of his calling.

The church's apostolicity pertains both to its life and its teachings since, especially in the Baptist tradition, the life of the redeemed and transformed community is conceived of as a definite part of its message. Guaranteeing the theological soundness of the minister is certainly not the whole method of maintaining the church's apostolicity. The church in any local congregation depends on the prayers, support, criticism, and intercession of the church in other local congregations to maintain its loyalty to the "faith once delivered." It is a distinct part of the executive secretary's responsibility to continue to implement this cross-flow of the Spirit in the life of the church. The local Baptist churches are not only united at the levels on which they do co-operative work, but are also united in Christ at the very heart of their lives, in their prayer, worship, proclamation, and service.

The catholicity or universality of the church demands of the executive secretary a continuous job of education. Local churches must constantly be reminded of their integral connection with the church in every land and age. Two suggestions might be included here. At the point of church membership ceremonies Baptists need some concrete symbol that the new members are part of something more than the local congregation, although this is where most of their lives as Christians will be lived. The practice of other denominations in having a figure who symbolizes the larger Christian community is instructive. Perhaps the executive secretary could become in Baptist practice the symbol of the church beyond the local church in which this membership is actualized. Also the use of traditional symbols of the Church Universal in past ages could be encouraged in Baptist churches. We believe that we are part of the church whose earthly life was lived in the Patristic Period, the Medieval Period, etc. The music and tradition of this portion of the Universal Church is just as much ours as anyone's. Its use would not only enrich worship, but help save Baptists from a temporal provincialism which sees back only at the very best, to the early American Baptists, the 17th century Baptists, or the Anabaptists, often ignoring the centuries of rich spiritual resources to which the Baptists are heir.

The oneness of the church is a characteristic which has suffered most at hands of Baptist polity. The mistaken notion of congregational "autonomy" which has in many places replaced the biblical and New Testament conception of the One Church expressed through the local churches has been most damaging. It is encouraging to see that co-operation and emphasis on the oneness of the church is a high concern of executive secretaries. Perhaps they will continue to lead Baptists into a further expansion of concrete expressions of the oneness of the church, not only in intra-denominational co-operation among local churches, but in the wider field of ecumenical co-operation and unity. The executive secretary who conceives his calling to the oneness of Christ's church mainly in terms of Baptist co-operation is operating on only one level and ignoring what is possibly the more important expression of the oneness of the church today.

The executive secretary's high calling as minister to the One, Holy, Apostolic, and Universal Church is a high one, with its commensurate demands for continuing self-examination and discipline.

This brings us to the second question, our Baptist Convention polity and the A.I.M. Report. One of the questions which the American Baptist Convention must answer within the next few years is the question of the organization of its denominational life. Are the present structures, relationships, and channels of communication the most appropriate for implementing the mission and unity of the denomination? At the request of the Convention a "management audit" was performed some time ago by The American Institute of Management. A report was published suggesting certain changes in the structure and practice of the various committees, agencies, and councils comprising the American Baptist Convention. The details of the Report are available but do not concern us here.

What does concern us is the theology behind such a procedure. First is the whole consideration of what is implied by the fact that a management audit agency was the first group consulted in the reorganization of the denomination. A management consultant cannot tell an organization what it should be or do; it can only advise it how to do what it wants to do more *efficiently*. Therefore, the consultation of the A.I.M. suggests that there was to be no basic theological evaluation of what the Convention is or should be, that the proposed reorganization would proceed simply on the basis that we clearly understand what we are, and that we just want to do better what we have been doing. We would like to suggest that before a managerial technique audit is evaluated, there must certainly be a previous theological agreement on what the denomination and the Convention *are*. Then, when there is a clear understanding of the mission of the denomination, an analysis of *how* this is to be done would be appropriate.

A second question grows out of the procedure by which the A.I.M. suggestions should or should not be accepted. The root problem here is this: On what basis will the recommendations be evaluated? Will they be studied in terms of a business organization seeking to maximize efficiency? Will they be thought of as procedural matters? Will there be some effort made to discover the theological implications of the A.I.M. Report? Will the final decision be made on the basis of a theology of the church which turns to business for technical and organizational advice? Or do we turn to business for resources on the basic polity and ecclesiastical structure of the denomination?

The trouble is there is no agreement on the Baptist understanding of the church. Until there is there can certainly never be any agreement on the basis by which the A.I.M. Report or any other is to be evaluated. Actually the A.I.M. Report clearly carries with it a contractual theory of the Church. The A.I.M. is certainly not to blame for this. All it had was the history of the gradual coming together of the various Baptist agencies in the last several decades. The A.I.M. consultants certainly did not use either the New Testament or the history and polity of the 17th century Baptists in their study. It suffers, therefore, from a tremendous chronological provincialism. Reorganizing the American Baptist Convention certainly cannot proceed simply on the basis of what the denomination is doing today and how its scattered agencies in the past decades have attempted to do their work. Since this is in fact what the A.I.M. Report attempts to do, it is necessarily based on incomplete data.

The possibility of a management audit of the Convention's organization raises the question of why a "theological audit" is not also possible. If the scattered and semi-autonomous agencies of the American Baptist Convention have proven to be inadequate to deal with the complex managerial problems of modern society, is it not also possible that the theological principles implicit in the denomination's life have also grown up out of response to other and now out-dated forces? If loosely-related agencies can be solidified into the staff and line organization suggested by the A.I.M., is it not possible that the principle of "local autonomy," appropriate perhaps to frontier society, can be re-evaluated as a basic premise in an age of mass society and centralized societal structures?

Therefore, we can only conclude that, prior to any evaluation of the A.I.M. Report, American Baptists need to have a far more basic consensus of what the Baptist denomination *is*. This is a theological question. The question must be settled and a consensus developed before any basis is present by which to evaluate such reports on organization. Meanwhile, it must be clearly understood that the A.I.M. Report, or any other similarly done, is *not* a "nontheological" one, but grows out of a particular theological understanding of the church, namely the contractual theory. This is obviously the theological basis for the present denominational structure. As such it falls far short of the New Testament.

Area Five: Baptists in Interdenominational and Ecumenical Movements

Believing as we do from our study of the New Testament that there are many sacred patterns of church order, not just one, we believe that Baptists should enter with both humility and conviction into interdenominational work and the Ecumenical Movement. To do so, however, we need theological understanding of our own free church order, where we agree and where we differ with other communions, and how we can contribute our particular insights to these movements. Suffice it to say here that it is our conviction that believing in the "gathered church" and the "ecumenical church" are never mutually exclusive. In terms of the theology of the New Testament presented above they are one and the same.

BIBLIOGRAPHY

Brunner, Emil, *The Misunderstanding of the Church*. Lutterworth Press, London: 1952, 132 pp.

Cook, Henry, *What Baptists Stand For*. London: Kingsgate Press, 1947, 188 pp.

Flew, Robert N., and Davies, Rupert E., *The Catholicity of Protestantism*. London: Lutterworth Press, 1950, 159 pp.

Jenkins, Daniel T., *The Nature of Catholicity*. London: Faber and Faber Ltd., 1946, 171 pp.

———, *The Strangeness of the Church*. Garden City, New York: Doubleday, 1955, 188 pp.

———, *Congregationalism: A Restatement*. London: Faber and Faber, 1954, 152 pp.

———, *The Church Meeting and Democracy*. London: Independent Press, Ltd., 1944, 63 pp.

Manson, Thomas W., *The Church's Ministry*. Philadelphia: Westminster Press, 1948, 114 pp.

VII

CHRIST AND MAN'S HOPE

———————◆—◆◎◆—◆———————

CHARLES R. ANDREWS

Let us not misunderstand our title. We do not refer to some "man's hope" which is inherently man's own, some indomitable spirit, some image of the divine, some inner integrity which gives hope in the midst of the fear—to which "hope" Christ has merely something to add, some encouragement, some enrichment to give. We know of no such adequate hope within ourselves; and we expect to run across no such hope (on any other basis than absent-mindedness) in anybody else. We can pull out all our pessimistic stops at this point, and let skepticism peal forth, forte-fortissimo. We are one with Faulkner and Tennessee Williams, Kafka and the later H. G. Wells in their worst nightmares. We accept the full implications of the cycle which began with the bright-eyed "Looking Backward" of Bellamy, and ended with the dully despairing "1984" of Orwell—and we accept this with some sense of relief. A live dog is better than a dead lion, and a true nightmare is better than a pie-eyed daydream.

We are interested in something else. We are interested in

Someone who actually twists this dark into light, who breaks again the broken back of this world, that it may be set properly and heal as it should. We sympathize with Walt Kelly's "in this dark, when we all talk at once, some of us must learn to whistle," [1] but we do not therein find the clue to the dissipation of night and the coming of dawn. We find the clue to the future, as we find the clue to the past and the present, in Jesus Christ.

So, for all we shall say about "man's hope," about some enthusiastic straining toward a shining goal, we shall attempt only to be talking about Christ, about what he has done and will do. We have no primary interest in some inner working of man's psyche; rather we have interest in an outer working of the plan of God—the manifestation of his loving purpose in Jesus Christ. If, through him, we are granted something called "hope", this is simply in the overflow of his grace, this is a by-product, this is not the real point. The real point is Christ: Christ's power, and Christ's will, and Christ's love. If we in some measure correctly interpret him, then this paper shall have achieved its purpose and our earnest prayer shall have been answered.

We have used the historical approach. We hope this is not simply because it tends to get us off the hook, allowing us to speak of what the Bible says, what early Christians and re-formers and liberals and neo-orthodox say, rather than forc-ing us to admit what *we* say. We frankly don't entirely know yet what we say; but we do feel that in a study of our past we shall be given at least some light upon our future. We have concluded, therefore, not so much with a well-polished statement of our hope neatly labeled for filing, but rather with a line of development and a list of problems, in wres-tling with which others may help us to say more precisely

---

[1] From *Potluck Pogo*, p. 181, by Walt Kelly; copyright 1954, Simon and Schuster, Inc., New York.

how it is that Christ—in this day—would have us to speak to the world of our hope in him.

I. HOPE IN THE BIBLE

A. *Hope in the Old Testament*

Although the word "hope" does not occur until late in the Old Testament, the covenant with God which undergirded Israel was itself the ground of hope, centering attention on what God had done in the past, was doing in the present, and had promised to do in the future.

The key to the understanding of Hebrew hope lies in the nature of the covenant and in the biblical understanding of time and history as under the Lordship of God. Time for the Hebrews can more nearly be called "filled time," concrete event, than merely abstract duration. Scott suggests that thought is centered upon the event or action in its conception, continuation, or completion. Time consists of the experience *in toto.* Both the past and the future are extensions of the present and are, therefore, present in the present. Since for the Hebrew the ultimate power of the universe was a personal, purposeful Lord who was directly known in the depths of human consciousness, it follows that if he is history's Lord, then history—time in its actual flow of events—is significant and purposeful.

As the Lord and Creator of time, God is not limited by finite conceptions of past, present, and future. He is quite able to declare things to us before they come to pass. In his will they have already happened! The role of the prophet is the divining and communicating of what God has already done in the transcendent realm but which has not yet become manifest in actual history: "My deliverance draws near speedily, my salvation has gone forth, and my arms will rule the peoples; the coastlines wait for me, and for my arm they hope" (Isa. 51:5).

The present is thus potent, ominous. Attention is riveted upon the future as it becomes present. In God's "declaring the end from the beginning . . ." (Isa. 46:10), we have the merging of past and future into the present which endows the present with such profound significance.

The prophetic announcement thus possesses a profoundly contingent quality, calling for ultimate decision. God declares his acts before they "come to pass" that their divine origin be unmistakable (cf. Isa. 48:5), and that his people have opportunity to respond to his message. Everything depends upon this response and there is no evading it. To respond in faith is salvation; to reject God's word is to incur judgment. In this situation—confrontation by transcendent necessity demanding radical obedience—the maximum in human effort is elicited. The degree of response becomes the measure of human fulfillment and freedom. This is the secret of the efficacy and inner dynamic of prophecy as well as the heart of its truth. Genuine prophecy "comes true" as people respond in faith and thus bring God's will to bear upon the concrete situations of history.

With this understanding of time and history under God's purpose, we may go on to consider specifically the covenant relation of Israel with God. This relation is characterized by three periods. First—the pivotal center of Hebrew history—is the complex of events comprising the Exodus, where the covenant was established and Israel was conceived as a holy nation. Second is the period of apostasy in which Israel has fallen away from the covenant and become submerged in the evil forces of history, and in which God presents "times" of possible redemption which are disregarded. We can understand Jeremiah: "Even the stork in the heavens knows her times; and the turtledove, swallow, and crane keep the time of their coming; but my people know not the ordinance of the LORD" (Jer. 8:7). The third and final movement of history for the Hebrews concerns the great intervention of God in Israel's life when he shall remake his chosen people and establish a new Israel. For Israel's apostasy had been so radical and her historical situation had become so tragically hopeless that the great prophets realized that only a new re-creating act of God would be able to repair the breach, reconstitute the Hebrews as a holy nation under God, and enable them to fulfill their promised destiny. In the shadow of this somber realization the covenant hopes of Israel became eschatological, reaching deepest and most sublime expression in Isaiah, chapters 40-55. Here in the very depths of despair, when the plight of Israel seemed utterly hopeless in the light of every possible historical circumstance, hope was affirmed with a deathless power, purity and meaning.

The foundation of this hope is the absolute omnipotence of God. Again and again, the prophet bases the capacity of God to redeem Israel on the fact that God is creator of heaven and earth, before whom the very nations are naught. He points to God's gracious deeds of the past, remembering God's promises of final redemption, his faithfulness, and his forgiveness of sins. That is, the disciple's angle of vision is turned toward the past where he may be reminded of the glory of God's nature and capacity to act, but only for the purpose of indicating that the future held not only possibilities like those of the past, but new, unheard-of possibilites.

The former things I declared of old, they went forth from my mouth and I made them known; then suddenly I did them and they came to pass. . . . You have heard; now see all this; and will you not declare it? From this time forth I make you hear new things, hidden things which you have not known. They are created now, not long ago; before today you have never heard of them, lest you should say, 'Behold I knew them' (Isa. 48:3, 6-7).

We then come to the point at which hope ceases to be merely future but becomes a redeeming reality of the present. When eyes of faith see that this salvation of God is "not far off" (Isa. 46:13), then God's activity will become manifest in history as well. Faith shall make God's promised acts come true in redemptive deed as well as in future promise. Life in the present becomes not only life lived in the light of God's promised future, but life lived as a *living expression* of this promise, or life lived *in* the promise. This gave birth to a whole range of eschatological joys which restored meaning to existence in the midst of despair and gave new strength to the poor in spirit. Present existence was redeemed, given ultimate meaning, and new resources were made available for actually bringing God's will into effective operation in historical events. As the prophet articulates this union of present and future: "Sing for joy, O heavens, and exult, O earth; break forth, O mountains, into singing! For the Lord has comforted his people, and will have compassion on his afflicted" (Isa. 49:13).

B. *Hope in the New Testament*

1. *The Advent of Christ as the Center of History*

The New Testament claims the advent of Christ as the supreme turning point of history and the final revelation of its ultimate meaning. The consummation of existence anticipated by the prophets had actually begun with the coming of the long awaited Messiah. The forces of darkness, death, and decay which had dominated the human situation since the Fall of Adam were now defeated by Christ and mankind was released from bondage:

> Then as one man's trespass led to condemnation for all men, so one man's act of righteousness leads to acquittal and life for all men (Rom. 5:18). For the law of the Spirit of life in Christ Jesus has set me free from the law of sin and death (Rom. 8:2).

In the hidden depths of history the root forces of evil had been decisively defeated by Christ; therefore, he had power and authority over Satan's agents, the demons: ". . . With authority he commands even the unclean spirits, and they obey him" (Mark 1:27). This victory, first manifest in Jesus' healing power, would eventually reveal itself in the transformation of all creation.

> For the creation waits with eager longing for the revealing of the sons of God; for the creation was subjected to futility, not of its own will but by the will of him who subjected it in hope; because the creation itself will be set free from its bondage to decay and obtain the glorious liberty of the children of God (Rom. 8:19-21).

And that the Kingdom had come, that Christ had conquered sin and death, was unmistakably verified to eyes of faith by the unprecedented outpouring of the Holy Spirit and the great new power of the Risen Christ within men. Echoes of this tremendous experience are heard in almost every verse of the Book of Acts. All barriers between the natural and the supernatural, between what the modern world distinguishes as fact and myth, are transcended in the attempt to express the unimaginable rich and abundant reality in which the early church lived.

2. *The Kairos and the Second Coming*

Equally vivid in the writings of the early church is the unshakable conviction that in Christ's coming a great cosmic process had been initiated which would press irresistibly onward to a catastrophic consummation of all history in which the hidden victory of God in Christ over the evil forces of existence would become manifest to all. This expected universal, cosmic transformation, alluded to in Paul's letter to the Romans, is typical of the New Testament as a whole and receives its classic expression in the Revelation of John.

This double movement, everywhere reflected in the pages of the New Testament, is expressed as the first and second comings. Christ has come and Christ will come. The Kingdom of God has come and the Kingdom will come. What does this mean? First, we must realize that the first and second comings were viewed by both Christ and the early church as inseparably bound up in the same event. As C. H. Dodd reminds us:

> The more we try to penetrate in imagination to the state of mind of the first Christians in the earliest days, the more we are driven to think of resurrection, exaltation, and second advent as being in their belief, inseparable parts of a single divine event. . . . They proclaimed it not so much as a future event for which men should prepare by repentance, but rather as the impending corroboration of a present fact. . . .[2]

Mark appropriately and significantly records the beginning of Jesus' ministry with the following announcement: ". . . the time is fulfilled, and the kingdom of God is at hand; repent, and believe in the gospel" (Mark 1:15). Remembering the Old Testament conception of time and history dealt with earlier in this paper, which is carried intact into the New, we may say that Jesus was heralding the dawn of a "new age," a new "time of fulfillment," a new *Kairos*. The meaning of this new *Kairos* with Christ finds its clearest expression in the writings of Paul. He teaches that with the coming of

---

[2] From *Apostolic Preaching*, p. 33, by C. H. Dodd; copyright, 1949, Harper & Brothers, New York.

Christ history is divided into two ages—the present age and the age to come. Further, upon all Christians: ". . . the end of the ages has come" (1 Cor. 10:11). This means two things: First, instead of the new age simply replacing the old age of sin and death, the old and the new age now co-exist alongside each other. Christians are those who have responded to the *Kairos* in repentance and have thereby entered into the new age. But, secondly, the new age contains within itself the seeds which will eventuate in its consummation. This is the end of history as both *finis* and *telos* which shall witness the final, catastrophic overthrow of evil, a universal resurrection to judgment and the creation of a new heaven and earth. The two ages overlap: the old age passing away, the new age destined to eventuate in the consummation of the *Kairos:* "For as in Adam all die, so also in Christ shall all be made alive. But each in his own order: Christ the first fruits, then at his coming those who belong to Christ. Then comes the end, when he delivers the kingdom to God the Father after destroying every rule and every authority and power" (1 Cor. 15:22-24).

In the Christian faith the *Kairos* expresses the synthesis of the eternal and the temporal. Therefore, in the *Kairos* God manifests himself in all his fullness. This is always true of God's economy as the logic of trinitarian thinking eloquently bears witness. So in the fulfillment of time (the *Kairos* as embodied in Christ's coming) appears the end of all history both as fulfillment of *telos* and eventual *finis*. For in Christ was full divinity, complete perfection, the union of actuality and potentiality. Consequently, Christ constituted the fulfillment of history—the consummation of *telos*—the ultimate meaning of history as it exhausts itself in actualization. This is the "end" in which the hidden supernatural goal of history is made manifest and which can, of course, be only mythically articulated by such passages as: ". . . and you will see the Son of man sitting at the right hand of Power, and coming with the clouds of heaven" (Mark 14:62).

For Paul, the *Kairos* brings with it not only a radical qualitative transformation of existence but just as radical a revision of the meaning of history. History acquires a new center and with this new center its culmination and fulfillment. The *Kairos* appears fully in one "moment" of history in the event of the Incarnation. Jesus Christ is the beginning and the end, for in Christ we see not only the fulfillment of the possibilities of finite existence, but the dawning of a new age and the invincible assurance of the triumphant consummation of history as well. Christ overcame death, was resurrected, and is now in the midst of his churches. He lives on and his anticipated return represents the personalization of the final culmination and consummation. The risen body of Christ is identified with the *Kairos* and the *Kairos* cannot realize itself completely within history except over a period of indefinite duration. And the indefinite character of this duration is part of the veil behind which God remains hidden from the eyes of man. "It is not for you to know times or seasons . . ." (Acts 1:7).

3. *The Unity of Time in Christ*

According to the unique biblical sense of time, the future can announce itself as present and become in a sense a present reality without the future losing its quality and genuine futurity. The words of W. Schweitzer remind us that the whole eschatalogical movement of the New Testament is centered in Christ:

> Eschatology is . . . concerned not so much with the "last things" as with him who is "the first and the last." This explains why in seeing him the New Testament witnesses were able to see the coming Kingdom as an already dawning re-

ality, and why the resurrection was the mainspring of faith in the second coming.[3]

The hope of the New Testament, then, is completely centered in what God in Christ has done, what the resurrected Christ is doing, and what Christ glorified will do. Christ has come, Christ is with us, and Christ will come. Further, these three aspects of "hope in Christ" belong fundamentally together in a unified whole and cannot be sundered from each other. The foundation of this unity is, of course, the unity of God and his complete Lordship over time and history.

4. Life in the Age to Come

Let us now examine the religious dynamics of the structure of hope in the New Testament. To Paul there are, in a sense, two meetings between the disciple and his Lord. The first takes place when the disciple, as the manifestation of God's election, steps from one age, the dying age, to the new age which Christ has ushered in, over which he now reigns, and which he will consummate and reveal to all at the end—the *finis* of time and history. Then all will be resurrected and judged—this is the second meeting. Yet although "the end is not yet", it nevertheless is breaking in upon the present in Christ's power. In this sense the future "end" has already become present. Christians are beginning to live in the "end time" which is yet to come. Thus the final fulfillment of history is also an ever-present quality of religious experience— an ever-present redeeming reality which lends purpose to life and arms the Christian with the power of an invincible hope. He is not only filled with the joy of the presence of Christ crucified; he is assured by this same presence of the ultimate certainty of the final redemption of history and nature. Inso-

---

[3] From *Eschatology and Ethics*, p. 7, by W. Schweitzer, ed.; Published by the Study Dep't of the World Council of Churches, 17 route de Malagnore, Geneva, Switzerland, Nov. 1951.

far as the Christian lives in the *Kairos* he lives at the juncture of the two ages—the old and the new. He lives in the union of the transcendental and temporal components of existence and in this "tension" the temporal imminence of the end becomes a function of the intensity of religious experience. It cannot be otherwise in this situation where *telos* and *finis* are intimately blended in the religious consciousness. This makes the intellectual juggling of emphasis upon the present *or* future Christ, sometimes indulged in, irrelevant to the religious experience of the early church. For in their experience these two aspects of the eschatological were in vital union. As far as the faith of the early church is concerned, the debate about their proper emphasis is as empty and misplaced as the misunderstanding of the relation between Christian freedom and moral behavior with which Paul had to contend in the church at Corinth.

Insofar as the Christian disciple lives by God's promise, he lives in the future as it impinges upon the present. This is possible because of the dual nature of God's relation to history—his being both within and beyond it, and his Lordship over time and history. Consequently, the prophets could announce God's word as genuinely future and yet as impinging, in "a little while," upon the present. So it was that the disciples of Christ could see in his coming the "first fruits" of a new age which had already dawned but which was yet to be consummated. This means that the consciousness of time is revolutionized. Man no longer lives from the past into the present, in the old age of sin and death where he must try to predict, plan, forestall and calculate according to his own desires, purposes, and ambitions. The disciple lives in the new age—the coming age—from the future as it flows into the present. This demands constant ultimate decision, humility, patience, trust, and expectancy, all in the context of God's continually confronting him with the demand of unconditional obedience.

But this does not even faintly suggest the abundance of joy that dominated this life in the "age to come." The joyful awareness of the presence of the Risen Christ among his churches and the invincible faith that he would soon finish his work more than amply supplied the strength and motive power to meet the rigorous demands of Christian discipleship. The coming of the Kingdom of God, God's loving and gracious gift through Christ destined to eventuate in the fulfillment of God's creation, was already seen to be bursting in and about the early Christians. Joyously these early pilgrims anticipated the final coming of their Lord, when all would be united with him in a transformed heaven and earth, and a glorious, eternal, resurrected fellowship finally established. It was this invincible and impregnable hope that armed the early Christians for their battle with the world, and which enabled them to overcome that world.

II. THE BIBLE MEETS THE GREEK WORLD

We see, then, that the outlook of the biblical writers is bright with hope: hope in Christ and his coming in glory, hope for a quite obvious and "down-to-earth" manifestation of God's Kingdom, a renovation of the universe, a new heaven and a new earth. In this their joyful prospect we might determine at least four elements:

1. The scene of the coming event was to be this universe in its *totality*. It was not "of this world" in the sense that it would come from this world; but neither was it "out of this world." God's Kingdom was and would be related to history.
2. But it was an expectation not simply historical in a general sense. It had become for Christians a personal

history, a personal work of Jesus Christ. This is why
New Testament eschatology is never merely a general
"doctrine of last things." Christian eschatology is the
expectation of *what Jesus Christ is going to do*. This
indicates the reason why the doctrine of Christ's "coming again" in glory is of importance: he it is who will
effect God's Kingdom upon this universe; its coming is
bound up with his person. "Jesus is the subject of the
New Testament religion. Eschatology is the predicate.
The subject is not subordinated to the predicate but the
predicate to the subject. Eschatology is made plastic to
Jesus Christ." [4]

3. Thus, Christians were men set on the verge of a new
age, with evidence of its near approach—the Spirit,
prophecy, love—all around them. It was breaking
through; extending itself on earth in the Church Body
of Christ. The response of men to this gracious new
setting in which God was placing them was glad thankfulness, spontaneous and joyful love, trusting faith.
Their characteristic service was a "eucharist," a "thanksgiving," and their day of worship represented not only
a memory of the resurrection "on the first day," but the
joyful expectation of "the eighth day, which is the beginning of another world." [5]

4. As a Kingdom brought by love wherein was thanksgiving, its nature was that of a community of persons, a
society of Christ with his people. Although details of
the hope might vary, a "kingdom" is, after all, a social
order. The basic theme of any hope for a kingdom is by
definition social rather than individualistic in nature.
This seems borne out by much of the New Testament.

---

[4] From *Eschatology*, p. 2, by William Manson, Scottish Journal of Theology
Occasional Paper No. 2; Oliver & Boyd, Ltd., Edinburgh.
[5] From *Epistle of Barnabas*, 13:9, c. A.D. 130.

The Kingdom was to be like the fellowship of a "marriage banquet" (cf. Matt. 25:1-13; Rev. 19:9), in a basically personal relation like that expressed today (following Buber) as the relation between "I and Thou." For the early Christians the immediate destiny of an individual soul after death was relatively unimportant, save as it would or would not participate in the coming Kingdom (cf. 1 Thess. 4:13-17). Even souls "in heaven" had to wait for the real consummation which yet lay ahead (cf. Rev. 6:10). Basically, the hope of both living and dead was for a corporate resurrection into a newly renovated heaven and earth, a society of God in the fellowship of Christ. Thus was the doctrine of the resurrection of the body important: the whole man, the whole personality, was involved in God's ultimate plan for the complete society of love on the scene of God's re-creation.

With this joyful proclamation that Christ would manifest his Kingdom and refashion creation, early Christians set out to face the world. But in some sense it was like advancing into a noxious fog. So pervasive was the Hellenistic atmosphere that it enveloped and all but smothered the unsophisticated Christian faith. The history of the post-Apostolic Church is a history of the at least partial dissolution of the Christian hope. Wherein the four elements we have discerned were radically altered by Hellenist thought appears when we itemize thus:

1. Since for a Hellenist, history and the events of the world had not the importance they had for the Hebrew Christian Church of an earlier day, since the Greeks conceived of the universe as a basically dualistic realm of "spirit" over against "matter," and since "the Greek conception of blessedness is thus spatial, determined by

the contrast between this world and the time-less beyond, (and) . . . not a time conception determined by the opposition between Now and Then" [6] the first element in the prospect of Christians—for the "Then" of the Kingdom to refashion the "Now" of the earth—was exchanged in Hellenistic thought for a Kingdom "above," to attain which one must ascend out of this lower world to the spiritual realms on high.

2. Likewise, a Hellenist could not expect from Christ what the New Testament had hoped. Inasmuch as the world was not to be saved but to be escaped, Christ could have no future to offer the world, no final recreation to effect upon it. His "return in glory" could have no real meaning or purpose to a Greek, and his work in Greek minds became that of opening a path of escape whereby men's spirits might ascend from the material world to the timeless kingdom of spirit. Here eschatology is no longer "plastic to Jesus Christ," but Jesus Christ has become plastic to the Greek worldview.

3. Further, the attitude of Christians toward the Kingdom was changed from joy over that which was coming upon them by the gracious love of God, to anxiety that they personally and individually attain the Kingdom, from trusting and thankful faith in what God in Christ had done and would do, to dutiful and nervous striving to be good. Their communion meal of expectant thanksgiving prefiguring the marriage feast of the Kingdom became merely a remembrance of their departed Lord; [7]

---

[6] From *Christ and Time*, p. 52, by Oscar Cullman; copyright, 1950, by W. L. Jenkins, The Westminster Press. Used by permission.

[7] A development which led eventually, "if the entering into it was to have any objective reality outside the mind," to the notion of the repetition of Christ's sacrifice and the parody of Christian faith which is the Mass. (Cf. Dom Gregory Dix, *The Shape of the Liturgy*, p. 305 and esp. p. 623, from which the phrase quoted is taken.)

and their "eighth day of worship," prefiguring the New Age, became a reversion to Sabbatarianism, with all the legalisms thereupon attendant.

4. And, finally, Hellenism bequeathed to the Church a hopelessly individualistic concept of the Kingdom. If the theme of salvation is the ascent of the soul to God, then the state of the individual soul after death becomes all-important, while the eventual "new heaven and earth" becomes anticlimactic. If the soul is already blissfully in heaven (or is already justifiably roasting in hell), what need is there for anything further? What point could there possibly be to Christ's return or the renovation of the universe? This inner contradiction has remained to plague Christians throughout the centuries.

And so we see that the commonly accepted picture of the "last things" which emerged from the Hellenist-Christian confrontation, and which came to characterize the later Christian outlook, although familiar to us, is rather different from the biblical hope. The normal picture rests in a Hellenistic frame. Heaven is "above," to be attained after death by the soul who "lives right." While this "heaven" may bear some relation to a society, its attainment is individualistic; this is not so much a doctrine of last things for the total creation as a doctrine of last things for the individual soul. The future work of Jesus Christ is changed from that of manifesting his Kingdom upon a changed earth to that of judging and rewarding the souls of men as they ascend the path up the heavenly steep which he has blazed for them to follow. In this framework the notion of a New Age to come seems quite peripheral; the future state of the material universe is of no great concern to the spirit which leaves it all for his heavenly home. This is a radical change from the view which found

heaven and earth waiting "with eager longing for the revealing of the sons of God" (Rom. 8:19), "groaning in travail together until now" (Rom. 8:22), with even the saints in
heaven looking ahead to the Day of the Lord, praying, "O
Sovereign Lord, holy and true, how long. . . ?" (Rev. 6:10).

For all the devotion and skill of the second-century Christians, they were not able to prevent this development, a development which they themselves furthered—albeit unwill-
ingly and unconsciously—with ramifications which extend
through the Dark Ages into the age of the Reformation, and
thence to us.

III. THE CHURCH ATTEMPTS ONCE MORE TO HOPE

A. *Biblical Reformation*

Since the Reformation was in its intention a return to the
Bible, a slashing behind the Greek-medieval world to the
Hebraic-Christian world, hope in the purposes of God—
weakened throughout the medieval period—naturally revived
among Reformed Christians. "The Reformation stands for
the rediscovery of the living God of the Bible, who actively
intervenes in the affairs of men, the Lord, and the Judge of
history, and with that comes a powerful realization of the
historical relevance of eschatology. Here we have a return
to the realist, historical perspective of Biblical eschatology
which envisages both a new heaven and a new earth, an ultimate end in which the fulness of the creation is maintained
unimpaired in union with a heavenly consummation." [8]

With Calvin, in particular, a robust eschatology sounds
forth. Whereas, with Rome, the Kingdom tended to be
wholly present in the Church, and whereas, with Luther, the

---

[8] T. Torrance, *Eschatology*, p. 38, Scottish Journal of Theology Occasional
Paper No. 2; *op. cit.*

Kingdom tended to be wholly future and unrelated to the Church, Calvin interpreted the Kingdom hope of Christians as having both present and future reference. He by no means thus [9] dimmed the glories of the Kingdom yet to come; rather, because of its identity with Christ, he found these glories to be prefigured in the present, even as Christ was now present with his church. That is, for Calvin the Kingdom has two aspects: it will come in glory to judge and renovate the earth; yet it has come in the lowliness of Christ, and by the union of the Church with him it advances into the actual mundane events of present life. Because the Christian sits on the resurrection side of the cross, by faith living with Christ in his Kingdom while yet on earth, the church can carry on its task of extending the Kingdom on earth. The present state of the Kingdom is lowly—the face of the church is humble even as Christ himself came humbly—but in its lowliness it is here through our union with Christ in the Spirit. Thus, "Calvin's eschatology was activist, stressing the mighty acts of God in Christ and *therefore* the work of the Church in obedience and joy, in thankful assurance of victory waiting for the final act of redemption." [10]

From this recognition of the Kingdom's presence in lowliness springs (and this is of particular importance for Baptists) Calvin's emphasis on Church discipline. Over and above the marks which Luther attributed to the Church—Word and Sacrament—Calvin (following Butzer) included the third mark of *discipline,* which makes the Kingdom visible (in its humility) in the Church on earth. "Discipline" must not here be understood in a narrow fashion; it includes

---

[9] While Calvin shows some confusion with regard to the full future hope of the Kingdom, it was not due to his emphasis on the present characteristics of the Kingdom, but rather, as will appear below, to certain Hellenist remnants in his thinking.

[10] T. Torrance, *op. cit.,* p. 55.

the total responsibility of the Church that her members personally live the Christian life, holding high standards of knowledge of the faith, prayer, stewardship, etc., while in terms of Church activity as a whole it implies not only correct teaching and preaching, but missions, social assistance, evangelism, order within the Church, and ecumenical concern.[11]

Only in one respect (and this unfortunately a serious one) may we say that Calvin's thought did less than justice to the Christian hope in Christ's future work. "The eschatology of Luther and Calvin lacks very largely the cosmic breadth which is characteristic of the Biblical expectation of the end. They fail to do justice to the ideas of the perfection of the new humanity as a whole, of the church in the coming kingdom of God and of the new creation in a new heaven and earth. It was not without reason that both Luther and Calvin were unable to deal with the Revelation of John." [12]

For all his excellences, Calvin could not free his mind from that Hellenist individualism with regard to the afterlife which finds the "immortal soul" slipping off at death into "heaven" for such a full life with the Lord that little point or purpose remains in the universal consummation of creation. This tragically weakened his hope for the future, since it is in clear contradiction to the biblical view—which, in his loyalty to Scripture, Calvin also tried to hold. "On the one hand the position of the soul after its emancipation from the body is described with the utmost fervor as the goal of all our hopes; on the other hand it is depicted as a yet incomplete state. It is at one and the same time already blessed and not yet so." [13] Although Calvin himself might be able to

---

[11] See both Torrance (*op. cit.*, pp. 61,62) and Quistorp, Heinrich; *Calvin's Doctrine of the Last Things,* Richmond, Va., 1955, pp. 125,126,179.

[12] Quistorp, *op. cit.*, pp. 12,13.

[13] *Ibid.*, pp. 81,82.

hold these warring conceptions at once in his mind without doing overmuch harm to his basically biblical outlook, his successors could not. The corporate hope dimmed as the individual hope overspread it. This inner contradiction was to become a source of great weakness in the Reformed tradition,[14] including English Independency, as we shall see. But, except for this serious flaw, we find in Calvin a real restoration of the biblical hope: a Kingdom which in Christ is to come in glory into history, yet on the verge of which Christians by their union with Christ stand in disciplined and humble fellowship, wherein is both watching and preparing for the ultimate perfection still to be manifested through Christ upon God's fallen world.

B. *Kingdom; Discipline; Baptists*

It is, in part, out of the emphasis of Calvinism on discipline within the church fellowship as it foreshadows the Kingdom's dawning, that the English Independent movement arose. Certain English Calvinists, confronted with a state church whose reformation had been more political than religious, and confronted at the same time by the demand of their Calvinist faith that the church be the eschatological fellowship noted by Word, Sacrament *and* discipline, were forced into a position of "reformation without tarrying for any"— gathering together in "separatist," or congregational churches. The Baptists were an integral part of this movement,[15] who, out of a study of the Bible *and out of the need*

---

[14] *Ibid.*, pp. 193-4.

[15] That they were essentially unrelated to the continental Anabaptists with which they are often confused is indicated by their Calvinist theological position (both in its Arminian and "orthodox" expression), by their church government (which is identical with the Congregational and quite different from, say, the Moravian), and by their own early and vehement protests against just such an identification with the Anabaptists as was being made by their opponents.

for discipline, became convinced of the necessity of believer's baptism as opposed to paedobaptism. It is well to emphasize that the Baptist movement arose not for the purpose of being obnoxious about the administration of one of the Christian sacraments, but rather arose out of the insight, backed by the testimony of the New Testament, that to ensure discipline and the showing forth of the Kingdom in the church, baptism could introduce into the church only believers (cf. esp. the Somerset Confession of 1656, Articles 25:2, and 26). The basic Baptist witness was simply a further step in the direction Calvin had set in his recognition of the church as the disciplined eschatological community.[16]

Thus we find in the early Baptist formularies a full understanding of the influx of the Kingdom into the world via the Church under the personal rule of Christ as king. The London Confession of 1644 reads:

> Touching his Kingdome, Christ being risen from the dead ascended into heaven; . . . having all power in heaven and earth given unto him, he doth spiritually govern his Church, exercising his power over all Angels and Men, good and bad, to the preservation and salvation of the elect . . . continually dwelling in, governing and keeping their hearts in faith and filliall feare by his Spirit. (art. 19)

This Kingdom is visible in the life and witness of the Church:

> Christ hath here on earth a spirituall Kingdome which is the Church, which he hath purchased and redeemed to himselfe as a peculiar inheritance: which Church as it is visible to us is a company of visible Saints, called and separated from the world by the word and Spirit of God, to the visible profession of faith of the Gospel, being baptized into that

---

[16] As the modern neo-Calvinist, Karl Barth, in his doctrine of baptism so well illustrates. See his *The Doctrine of the Church Concerning Baptism.*

faith and joyned to the Lord and each other by mutuall agreement in the practical injoyment of the Ordinances commanded by Christ their head and King. (Art. 33)

But this is true only as discipline is rightly administered, as Christians "lead their lives in Christ's walled sheepfold and watered garden to have communion here with the Saints, that they may be made to be partakers of their inheritance in the Kingdome of God" (Art. 39), baptizing into the fellowship only "persons professing faith" (Art. 39), upholding Christian standards (Art. 35) and, if need be, excommunicating (Art. 42) "with care and tendernesse" (Art. 43).

The delicate instrument for the exercise of the rule of Christ was the church meeting, where by prayer and the Spirit, the congregation—the covenant community—might come to a true knowledge of the will of Christ, where, then, the Kingdom could break through most brilliantly and most concretely, issuing in love among the brethren and in power toward the world.

It is curious that, with this intense fellowship and discipline within the local church, rooting in the very corporate concept of the Kingdom's presence through the personal Kingship of Christ at work among believers, Baptists should have become—in rather short space of time—so tragically individualistic as to compromise gravely the fervent corporate hope implicit in their early creeds.

At least in part, this curiosity is to be explained firstly by that Hellenistic strain in Calvinism wherein an individual heavenly destiny counterbalances and eventually erases the corporate hope of the Kingdom. At this point the Bible was increasingly neglected and the Hellenist-medieval ascent to heaven increasingly assumed. Attention came to be turned from the free acceptance of the grace of God who in Christ elects men into his Kingdom, to the anxious and spiritually contaminating question "Will I get into heaven?" and to breathless "works" to prove this a possibility. Unfortunately (but naturally) the early Baptist creeds themselves carry on Calvin's individualizing tendency. Although unexceptional in proclaiming the Kingdom's present power in the Church for renovation, they are extremely one-sided in their thoughts on its future power in the universe. Except in the great Calvinist London Confession of 1644 (Art. 20) and in certain Arminian Baptist creeds (Confession of 1660, Art. 22; Orthodox Confession of 1678, Art. 23—and here with reservations!) Baptist anticipation has far less to do with the renovation of heaven and earth through the loving will of God in Christ, than with the reception into "heaven" of the elect (us!) and the casting into "hell" of the reprobate (them!).

Coupled with this rebirth of the old medieval synthesis, a tragic development peculiar to Baptists occurred. In its inception, believer's baptism had corporate as well as individual reference, in that it not only signified the faith of the believer but also the purity of the faith of the community, safeguarding it as far as possible from adulteration by nominal Christians, ensuring church discipline and thus, also, the manifestation of the Kingdom in the present life of the church. So obstinate, however, was the church at large in recognizing this, so distinctive did this practice become of "Baptists" alone, that believer's baptism was torn from its subordinate position as a safeguard of discipline to become among Baptists a law, a work, an end unto itself. As it became more and more important in itself, it tended to lose that purpose which subordinated it to more important aspects of the faith: its function as a sub-head under discipline, which itself was a sub-head under the manifestation of the Kingdom among men. Instead it retained only that meaning which made it important in itself: the showing forth of the faith of the believer.[17]

To say this, of course, does not tell the whole story. Baptists, with other denominations, were inundated with the deluge of pietist revivalism.[18] That this might have been stemmed, or ridden victoriously by a denomination sure of its own purpose, is a moot question. But with the internal weakening of the foundations, Baptists were in no condition to channel successfully the Methodist revival, to use it creatively for the unique purposes of Baptists. They simply swam with the tide, extending their name successfully to all points of the new American land, but losing connection in the process with the original purpose which had called them out for separate witness.

For these reasons, therefore, from being the sign equally of the believer's faith and of his incorporation into the Church with its discipline, baptism became the sign of the former alone. Thus it became an individualistic rather than a corporate act, a subjective rather than an objective act, wherein the faith of the soul became more important than the grace of the God who creates faith and fashions it into the fellowship of the church. Ultimately "faith" itself became so predominantly subjective—a thing to be evoked from

---

[17] Compare the Somerset Confession of 1654, wherein by baptism the believer is "being planted in the visible church or body of Christ" (Art. 24) with the New Hampshire Confession of 1833, wherein the purpose of baptism is "to show forth in a solemn and beautiful emblem, our faith. . ." (Art. 14).

[18] We must be careful in our day not to become angry with pietism. It was without question a valid correction of petrified "orthodoxy." Someday, when we have secured our present advances, we may no doubt look with more favor on its fervid faith. Nevertheless we can never forget that in its total impact it served to disrupt certain of the corporate and communal aspects of Christianity in favor of a rather subjective and emotive "faith." Possibly had pietism taken a different turn it would not have been as successful, but it might have left among evangelical Protestants a more relevant Christian message for the problems of the twentieth century. This message we are only beginning to rediscover in the concerns of our earlier forebears.

within rather than a response to Him who confronts one from without—that the disastrous forcing of spurious emotion ensued, one of the worst aspects of degenerate revivalism.

Like a house built in one lot when its foundation has been laid in another lot—a poor manner of construction—the Baptist denomination, having as its foundation the rocklike expectation of the renewal of creation in a Kingdom which even now was foreshadowed in the disciplined church of Christ, was nevertheless erected elsewhere—on the sands of individualism, ascent to heaven, and anxious search for salvation.

Practically speaking, this might be held to have been advantageous. Baptists swept the country, opened the wilderness, extended that rather irresponsible freedom known as "rugged individualism." It was the tenor of the times, and numerically Baptists rapidly increased.

For its success, however, the Baptist denomination paid with its soul. Its theological losses were immense. Its initial reason for existence was forgotten. Its hope tended to become non-historical and "heavenly," its faith to be placed in the half-Christ who judges souls but who does not overcome the world, its interest to be shifted from the grace of God who is *agapē* to the erotic ascent to heaven. From the community of faith to the individual of rectitude, from the thanksgiving of the adopted sons of God to the energetic thrashing of the sinking sinner, from the *acceptance* of God to the *search* for God, this was the direction taken. The Holy Communion had little chance to flower into glad expectation of the Kingdom. Taking the opposite pole from Rome it became a merely memorial meal, a subjective "remembrance," observed only because—for some obscure reason—Christ had ordained it. Discipline slowly relaxed as the sense of community disintegrated and as the Church Meeting declined. Thus developed the curious anomaly of a fellowship which in its first

and valid impulse had been called out to be the eschatological community, tending to lose its eschatology! With this
loss, only two options remained: either the Baptist group
could become a pietist sect unrelated to history—individuals
trudging their self-righteous path to heaven—or it could
become a social-action lobby unrelated to the gospel—individuals hurrying to tidy up the world. We shall see as we
proceed that both are being tried. Neither is particularly
interesting or biblical.

A third path is open to us. But it entails a revival of hope
in the Kingdom which Christ is to bring upon the world—a
new society coming by the outpouring love of God to con-
demn and renovate creation, on the verge of which we are
joyfully set by our incorporation into the disciplined community wherein the Kingdom (in its humility) is now at
hand. Whether we can move from our present denominational structure—set in great degree on individualism and
moralism—to build on our proper foundation—the corporate
hope of the Kingdom reign of God—God alone can know.

IV. THE IMPACT OF LIBERAL THOUGHT
ON THE CHRISTIAN HOPE

From what has been said of the "activist eschatology" of
Calvin, it should be clear that the seeds of a valid religious
and social "liberalism" lie at the heart of historic Baptist
belief and the Reformed tradition in general. In fact, it may
be that one of the few real excuses for the rise of a "liberal"
movement within the body of Christ's Church lies here—in
its character as a return to Calvin's belief that the Kingdom's
extension into the present is a fact of Christian life in the
Church.

Liberalism was, however, an amalgam of many forces
other than that of Calvin. A new land was to be won in

America. New principles had to be formulated upon which the new society might be firmly established in a new land. It required only the impact of new philosophical and scientific ideas of human progress to turn the spirit into a dynamic movement towards an applied Christianity for the realization of the ideals of the Kingdom of God in a reinvigorated society.

These ideas, generally summed up under the heading "evolutionary optimism," include a broad range of thought. The individualism of Locke, finding later expression in Jeffersonian contributions to democracy; the romanticism of Rousseau and his followers setting the unusual and adventurous over against the habitual and the commonplace while stressing also the inherent goodness of child-nature and the right of free expression; the philosophy of Hegel positing inevitable advance by thesis, antithesis, and synthesis; the transcendentalism of Kant reflected in an Emerson of a later date; the subjectivism of Ritschl and Schliermacher pointing to individual religious experience as a dependable and all-sufficient guide to spiritual truth; and the critical approach of Harnack describing the core of Christianity as the teaching of Jesus; all of these and other concepts gave new significance to the individual, questioned old authorities, and gave a new incentive towards exploration, invention, and scientific inquiry.

Also, the idea of the development of natural science advanced by Darwin and his successors together with Spencer's idea of human institutions as the products of slow growth contributed immeasurably to the notion that progress in the individual and in society was not only possible but inevitable. The laissez-faire doctrine of economics as implied in its Italian form "Il monde va da se" (The world goes by itself) added more degrees of optimism; and the rise of superior technical knowledge supported by a growing sense of national importance gave to the Western world, and to America in particular, such an unbounded confidence in the individual and his institutions as must sooner or later make its impact upon religious thought.

The members of churches scattered throughout the land, especially of those churches whose principles encouraged or at least allowed persons to exercise the spirit of free inquiry, could hardly fail to be influenced by the new cultural transformations taking place in industry, science, and philosophy and spreading by the rise of free public education. Creeds of the churches might not undergo immediate change but many of those who recited them would do so, sometimes consciously, sometimes otherwise.

The work of Paulus, Baur, and Troeltsch in Germany by way of close scrutiny of biblical literature, marked the beginning of such a process as it related to the interpretation of the Scriptures, a process that soon made its impact on scholars throughout the world (though making its way only very slowly with the laity and with many of the clergy) in the form of both new doctrinal formulations of Scriptural truth and new applications of the truth as thus reshaped.[19]

All Protestant bodies were affected more or less by these liberal socializing forces, Baptists among them. Baptist rejection of state control of the church compelled the local congregation to rely increasingly on the capacity for private judgment with a consequent freedom denied members of those religious bodies which were subservient to civic au-

---

[19] Though not the leaders in biblical criticism, Baptists were not wholly wanting in the spirit of inquiry in some other phases of religious development where they were actually leaders. We may remind ourselves that it was William Newton Clarke in this country, a Baptist teacher and writer, in his *Outline of Theology*, who was one of the first to carry the liberal approach over into the realm of Christian doctrine. And it was another Baptist, as we shall see in a moment, who became the leading exponent and dynamic inspiration for a careful inquiry into the practical bearings of the Christian faith upon the life of the times.

thorities or hierarchical systems of Church government. Since Baptists were generally of the humbler types of work-a-day citizens (in many cases immigrants from Europe) they were receptive to more liberal social attitudes; since they were foremost amongst religious bodies in following the pioneers into the new communities of the west, they were faced with the question as to what their gospel had to do with establishing the right kind of community. This evangelical spirit and missionary zeal that eventually pushed American Baptists (with Judson and Rice) beyond even the pioneer lands of the west, into the far reaches of the world, found this denomination leading in the task of breaking down the ills of poverty, sickness, ignorance, and oppressive systems of caste.

Perhaps no accident, therefore, brought it about that in America, it was a Baptist teacher and minister, who gave new shape to the Christian hope in the form of the Social Gospel; providing not only the stimulating idea, but also the initial driving power of a dynamic new movement that for decades and possibly for centuries to come will cause the American type of Christianity to be characterized as "practical" or "activist." Walter Rauschenbusch epitomized the influence of liberalism throughout the period of American expansion so far as it related to social issues; and he bequeathed to future generations a practical and humane aspect of Christian hope that would not forsake it even when the liberal point of view should face severe criticism as in our day.

Prevailing doctrines of Christian hope in the pre-liberal period, having chosen to retain only the Hellenistic aspect of Calvin's hope, emphasized man's need of individual redemption, and asserted that God through Christ had only made it possible for man to be saved *from* this world with all of its contradictions and confusions. Liberal thought now returned in part to the biblical side of Calvin's hope, and declared that God in Christ was also saving men *in* this world. Hence arose the dual type of citizenship that had been present in the earliest days of the gospel, but had been shied away from, if not altogether rejected, by an "orthodoxy" that had become unduly absorbed in "other-world" aspects of the faith. The Kingdom of God, as it came now to be defined, could not fail to embrace within it, along with the idea of the redemption of the individual, also the idea of the transformation of social conditions to make the will of God and the spirit of Jesus become regnant in human society.

This emphasis, however, was not without its difficulties. Loosed from the guiding spirit, the glowing faith and the deep religious experience of this giant prophet, the social emphasis had all the possibilities of turning into a brand of socialism and totalitarianism that would reject its Christian safeguards, as we now know they were rejected in later Communistic and allied movements in this and other countries of the world.

A more subtle and perhaps for that reason a more devastating danger of this "reform-the-present-world" point of view was the exaggerated note of optimism that often accompanied it. Liberalism in its numerous forms led easily to the notion that our ills are mostly a matter of bad environmental conditions and that our chief task is to clear out the slums to provide proper recreational facilities, to give every person complete freedom to develop his innate capacities, and to remove all chains of oppression. Then the Golden Age of Plenty will have arrived; the perfectibility of human nature will have been achieved; and the will of God will have been done on earth as it is in heaven.

Such unbounded confidence in human nature produced a new set of ideals that often received ready acceptance as a new way of life if not a new type of religion. Man came to feel that he could have here and now what was coming to him, if he developed his own powers and shaped his destiny according to inherent powers of progress, abetted by a world full of an abundance of "things" considered to be the *sine qua non* of happiness and the basis for the fulfillment of personality.

As a consequence, the ideas of the abiding sinfulness of man were widely ignored or rejected, with the result that news of the gospel ceased to be the announcement of a divinely and sacrificially achieved deliverance from sin and death, and became rather a declaration of a guiding spirit and principles by which an essentially good people could achieve a more nearly complete expression of selfhood in this world here and now.

Over against this easy optimism the cataclysmic developments of the twentieth century brought a widespread hunger for a more penetrating approach to what was increasingly felt to be the desperate plight of man's spiritual life. Liberal religion found itself in an uneasy seat and wondered whether it had within itself the strength and resources to meet this new demand. A search began for a more thoroughgoing understanding of the gospel to deliver man from his sorry estate. To this phase of the matter we shall now turn our attention.

V. THE RISE OF CONTEMPORARY THEOLOGY

Although the hopeless chaos of modern times, in shaking earlier complacency, prepared men for new ventures into the gospel message, it is crucial in our discussion to understand that the revival of interest in eschatology in the past half-century roots not primarily there—in the chaos—nor, certainly, in literalist fundamentalism, but rather in the development of a most radical kind of biblical criticism. It was Albert Schweitzer who in 1906 dealt the death blow to earlier conceptions of the "Jesus of History" and initiated the modern discussion. He defined the issue clearly in the following brief quotation:

> The Jesus of Nazareth who came forward publicly as the Messiah, who preached the ethic of the Kingdom of God, who founded the Kingdom of Heaven upon earth, and died to give His work its final consecration, never had any existence. . . . This image has not been destroyed from without, it has fallen to pieces, cleft and disintegrated by the concrete historical problems which came to the surface one after another, and in spite of all the artifice, art, artificiality, and violence which was applied to them, refused to be planed down to fit the design. . . . The thoroughgoing skeptical and the thoroughgoing eschatological school have only completed the work of destruction by linking the problems into a system. . . . [20]

Schweitzer held that Jesus had proclaimed a coming catastrophic event in the immediate future, and concluded that since his "future" has long since become our past, his view was an illusion. If the church was to have any confidence, let alone an absolute hope, in its Lord, Schweitzer's challenge could not go unheeded.

The struggle of modern theology with regard to eschatology is, thus, essentially an exegetical problem, making necessary the tools of careful biblical study. C. H. Dodd has stated most consistently the antithesis to Schweitzer's thesis. While admitting the collapse of the "modernizing" view, in his "realized eschatology," Dodd premises that in Jesus Christ the Kingdom has already become reality, and that both judgment and salvation are executed in the present. Eschatology is here not so much concerned with the future as with the significance of the present under the timeless rule of Christ.

---

[20] From *The Quest of the Historical Jesus*, p. 396, by Albert Schweitzer; copyright, 1948, The Macmillan Co., New York.

Roughly speaking, the views of the early Barth,[21] Bultmann,[22] and Tillich [23] represent similar attempts to deal with the problem Schweitzer poses.

Neither the "thoroughgoing" nor the "realized" eschatological school has in itself, however, seemed satisfactory to meet the question of man's hope for the future and its relevance to the present. In some ways we may say that in these days a synthesis—constructed upon the two extremes—is emerging, premising a kingdom already present and yet still to come. "Discussions as to whether the Kingdom is present or future are barren; it is obviously both." [24] "Jesus can only be the coming Messiah if He is the presently real Messiah—and vice versa." [25] Christ—his incarnation-crucifixion-resurrection—is the single, unrepeatable event in history. He

---

[21] "Knowing that the eternal 'Moment' does not, has not, and will not enter in, we should . . . become aware of the dignity and importance of each single concrete temporal moment, and apprehend its qualification and its ethical demand. Then we should await the Parousia: we should, that is to say, accept our present condition in its full seriousness; we should apprehend Jesus Christ as the Author and Finisher; and then we should not hesitate to repent, to be converted, to think the thought of eternity, and therefore . . . to love." From *The Epistle to the Romans*, p. 501, by Karl Barth; Oxford University Press, London, 1950.

[22] "Though Paul still expects the end of the old world to come as a cosmic drama that will unfold with the imminent parousia of Christ . . . that can only be the completion and confirmation of the eschatological occurrence that has now already begun. For with the sending of Christ 'when the fulness of time has come' it decisively began, so that it can already be said now: 'the old has passed away, behold, the new has come' . . . In the 'word,' the salvation-occurrence is present." From *Theology of the New Testament*, Vol. I, pp. 306-307, by Rudolf Bultmann; copyright, 1952, Charles Scribner's Sons, New York.

[23] " 'Kairos,' the 'fulness of time' . . . describes the moment in which the eternal breaks into the temporal, and the temporal is prepared to receive it. What happens in the one unique kairos, the appearance of Jesus as the Christ, i.e., as the center of history, may happen in a derived form again and again in the process of time." From *The Protestant Era*, p. xix, by Paul Tillich, copyright, 1948, University of Chicago Press.

[24] From *Realm of Redemption*, p. 223, by J. R. Nelson; quotation of Vincent Taylor; copyright, 1951, The Seabury Press, Greenwich, Conn.

[25] *Ibid.*, quotation of W. D. Wendland.

is at once the center, judge, and meaning of it all. At the same time the biblical concept of time understands the future plan of God as impinging on the present in redemptive power when heard with faith. For these reasons the present may be seen as a part of the future that has already begun in Christ, but which has not yet been consummated, has not yet been entirely "heard." The present stands under the Lordship of Christ, a situation which is not now obvious but which will one day be manifest to all. As Barth now puts it, expounding the petition "Thy Kingdom come":

> We pray for the removal of this covering which now conceals all things, as the cloth which covers this table (here he indicates a table covered by a cloth). The table is underneath (he raps on the table). You hear it. But you do not see it. You have only to remove the cloth to see it. We pray in order that the covering which still veils the reality of the Kingdom be removed, in order that the reality of everything already changed in Jesus Christ may be made visible.[26]

Cullmann expresses this [27] in terms of the period between D-Day and V-Day; between the time when the decisive battle of the war is fought, and the time when "mopping-up operations" are over and the final victory is won. With the crucifixion, the decisive event became factual history; the end was initiated and will be fulfilled in the final victory (parousia). The hope of V-Day is assured by D-Day. The hope of the Christian for the fulfillment of God's purpose is assured by Christ. The Christ who was, is our hope for what will be, the expression of God's final goal for his creation. Or as Nygren puts it:

> The gospel is the proclamation of the work wrought by God when He sent Jesus Christ into the world. It is the

---

[26] From *Prayer*, p. 49, by Karl Barth, translated by Sara F. Terrien; copyright, 1952, by W. L. Jenkins, The Westminster Press. Used by permission.

[27] Cullman, *op. cit.*, especially p. 141.

message about the dynamic activity which God thereby introduced into our existence. The gospel is the declaration that God brought something wholly new into this age, that through Christ he brought the new age among us—an age begun in our midst, but to be fulfilled in glory.[28]

How may we characterize this? What is this happening which is yet to be manifested? Briefly we may give content to our hope. Christ who is risen is "seated at the right hand of God" with authority over the world; we believe in the future kingdom of God because we believe in the present reign of Christ.

As we know our risen Lord, we know the purpose which God has for this world; we know not only that there is a divine ordering of history, but we know that the world is being ordered to conform to him, being re-created into his image (who himself is the express image of God), and we know that the power, the justice, the love and the mercy we find in him is the revelation of God's will for the world, even as he is God's agent for its accomplishment upon the world. He reigns in the "now" and will bring to completion his fulfillment in the "then." Further, since he is the key to the future, and is choosing a covenant people, we know that this is much more than salvation of individuals only. We may look forward to the resurrection of his corporate Body (of which his resurrection was the "first fruits") as he who came to save men comes again to redeem the world. Humanity and the individual cannot be artificially separated; the hope of the *world* is the Christ who reveals and fulfills. At the same time we cannot posit an easy and universal salvation; choice is required of us, either for the life which is in him or for the death which is everywhere else. The future glory becomes a present reality only as faithful response to the divine

---

[28] From *Commentary on Romans,* p. 25, by A. Nygren; copyright, 1949, Muhlenberg Press.

action is given . . . in repentance, commitment, and obedience.

Thus we must come to the conclusion that any "hope" in which Christ is not central is worthless. If man is dependent upon a God who is "outside" his mundane experience—and where is God within the world, in the flesh, to be heard, seen, looked upon and touched (cf. 1 John 1:1) save in Jesus the Christ?—he is like a drowning man in sight of land but unable to reach it. Christ is our hope—a hope that reveals God present above the tensions of this age, directing, sustaining and redeeming.

We find, then, that the eschatological setting into the recognition of which Schweitzer catapulted an unwilling and reluctant Church has, through painstaking study, both biblical and theological, not destroyed the confidence of the Church in its Lord. Rather is our confidence, our trusting hope, made far more clear, as is also the mission of the Church.

Hence, we have a hope to proclaim . . . a hope that is in God and revealed in Christ. Indeed, that hope *is* Christ in whom God is revealed as the Lord of history. God has in love established the "now" of this age over which Christ reigns (despite continuing but limited opposition of earthly powers). And God will, through Christ who is our hope, give us the "then" when he "has put all things in subjection under his feet" (1 Cor. 15:27).

OUR HOPE FOR BAPTIST THEOLOGY

We have come the long way round to our conclusions—via historical study. We find we have been quite selective; many problems we have left to one side for the present; this we readily admit. Our purpose has been, however, to trace in context a certain line of development which we feel will be fruitful for Baptists in particular to consider in this stage of biblical and ecumenical progress.

The line of development we have traced, and to which we wish to direct attention may be outlined as follows:

1. We have found the biblical view of time to be one wherein the future—as that which has already happened in the heavenly sphere—enters the present as it is accepted in faith; we have found that we thus are placed in every present in a state of intense expectation, that the Kingdom of God as the complete will of God for his creation presses in Christ upon us, ready to come into our midst, indeed, already partially present as we stand in faith before the loving Son of God among his brethren.

2. We have found this biblical expectation seriously compromised as it was diluted by the Hellenistic concept of a "future" which not only is separated from the present, but which is not expected to enter the temporal sequence at any point, which stands "above" in a higher sphere, haughtily inattentive to the earthly process.

3. We have found that insofar as Calvin understood the Kingdom as extending into the world through the church, and insofar as Baptists rightly held to believer's baptism as a means by which to ensure, through the purity of the church, precisely this Kingdom extension, the Reformation was a return to the biblical perspective. Insofar, however, as Calvin (and Baptists) misunderstood the character of the ultimate Kingdom, retaining a degree of Hellenistic spiritualism, the Reformation failed in its purpose, eventually losing (in pietism and later "orthodoxy") even the valid hope for the partial presence of the Kingdom with which it had begun.

4. We have found that liberalism in its initial stage rightly

regained Calvin's emphasis on the Kingdom's potential for expression in the present, albeit not without danger of losing the dimension of God's power in Christ whereby this expression might be made.

5. And we have found that biblical criticism and the biblical theology which this has initiated have made possible once more a full appreciation of the biblical expectation—the tension between that which is finally to come in Christ and that which has already come in Christ, between V-Day and D-Day—allowing the Church once more to be the community of hope, the place where the Kingdom is accepted, proclaimed, and (in its humility) entered, wherein the Kingdom which is yet to come, comes.

We feel that we arrive at a point of distinct interest for Baptists, at a point where Baptists through their unique witness have a very real contribution to make to the church at large. We hope, then, that studies in depth can be made in at least the following areas:

1. The nature of our Calvinist heritage. We feel that to know where we are going we must know whence we come.

2. The nature of the church as the community of joyful hope, of expectant believers, of intense brotherly love on the local and visible level of the gathered assembly of God. In their doctrine of the visible church as the actual gathered community, Baptist and other congregationalists have a distinct opportunity for offering a treasure to fellow Christians.

3. The nature of the two sacraments as expressions of hope, wherein communion is seen not only as "remembrance" but as expectation, and wherein believer's baptism is not only a symbol of individual faith but a

safeguard of the Kingdom's entrance into the church. We are aware of the usual Baptist apologetic that baptism of believers is "a more meaningful symbol," "expressive of faith," and the like, but we suspect that it is rather indecent for Baptists to exist as a separate entity, to be put on public display, in attire as theologically scanty as this.

4. The nature of the final hope to which we look. We would not concentrate solely on the expression of the Kingdom in our midst, as if characteristics of the Kingdom which is to come were unimportant, lest we unwarily fall again into the Hellenistic trap which held our forefathers. We would seek understanding of an eternity which comes to fulfill time, of a social Kingdom of believers with their Lord. We ask not for the precise arrangement of "heaven", but for the intimations we are given in Christ by which we may know what does and what does not belong to our ultimate hope in him (e.g. resurrection of the body vs. immortality of the soul, second advent and judgment of Christ vs. the free flight of the spirit to paradise).

5. But basic to it all, we call for study of the nature of time, feeling that such a pursuit might well issue in lines of thought more christologically significant for our day than are the traditional Greek categories of "substance" and "nature." If our interpretation of "hope" in the New Testament is correct, we find ourselves dealing not with static, abstract theories and categories, but with time-consciousness and eschatology, with cosmic movements and ultimate decision. The "second coming" is not simply an external appendage to the Christian faith. However we interpret it, it goes right to the very center of the "good news," completing the meaning of human life and history, affirming their ultimate

unity and redemption, and guaranteeing the final victory of good over evil.

BIBLIOGRAPHY[29]

Cullman, Oscar, *Christ and Time*. Philadelphia: The Westminster Press, 1950, 253 pp.

Dodd, Charles H., *The Apostolic Preaching*. New York: Harper & Bros., 1951, 96 pp.

McGlothlin, William J., *Baptist Confessions of Faith*. Philadelphia: American Baptist Publication Society, 1911, 368 pp.

Manson, Lampe, Torrance, and Whitehouse, *Eschatology*. Scottish Journal of Theology Papers No. 2. Edinburgh: Oliver and Boyd, 1953.

Marsh, John, *The Fulness of Time*. New York: Harper & Bros., 1952, 189 pp.

Minear, Paul S., *Christian Hope and the Second Coming*. Philadelphia: The Westminster Press, 1954, 220 pp.

Quistorp, Heinrich, *Calvin's Doctrine of the Last Things*. London: Lutterworth Press, 1953, 200 pp.

Torrance, Thomas, *The Doctrine of Grace in the Apostolic Fathers*. Edinburgh: Oliver and Boyd, 1948, 150 pp.

Whitehouse, Walter A., *The Christian Hope and the Task of the Church*. New York: Harper & Brothers, 1954.

---

[29] Certain paragraphs in this chapter have been previously published in *Theology Today*, for Jan., 1957, and are used here by kind permission of the editors.